VW BEETLE

TYPE 1 & THE NEW GENERATION

About the Author

By any standards, William Boddy is the doyen of motoring writers, for he was Editor of the British magazine *Motor Sport* for fifty years, still contributes to its pages, and has now been writing about cars since 1930.

Made famous for his trenchant and outspoken opinions in *Motor Sport*, and many other publications, 'WB' soon built up a large following, so when this British expert bought and championed the early VW Beetles, this caused a real stir.

William Boddy is now well into his eighties. Although he was originally apprenticed to Kings Autocars, and served with the Ministry of Aircraft Production during the war, he then revived and ran *Motor Sport*, and still found time to write a number of books, including the authoritative history of the Brooklands race track.

Awarded the MBE for his services to sports journalism in 1997, he now lives in mid-Wales.

OSPREY EXPERT HISTORIES

VW BEETLE

TYPE 1 & THE NEW GENERATION

WILLIAM BODDY

First published in Great Britain in 1982 by Osprey Publishing,
Elms Court, Chapel Way, Botley, Oxford OX2 9LP

Revised edition published Spring 1999

ISBN 1 85532 885 2

Editors: Tim Parker, Shaun Barrington
Associate Michael Sedgwick
Design: Fred Price
New colour section and new chapter design: The Black Spot
Jacket photography by Andrew Morland
Photography by Mirco Decet, Andrew Morland
With thanks to David Hodges for the loan of the 1938 VW brochure

Thoughts on the new Beetle have been kindly provided by Graham Robson.

New sections origination: Valhaven Ltd, Isleworth, UK
Printed through Worldprint Ltd, Hong Kong

99 00 01 02 03   10 9 8 7 6 5 4 3 2 1

Other titles published by Osprey Automotive include:

MG by McComb, third edition updated by Jonathan Wood
   ISBN 185532 831 3
Aston Martin 1913-1947, Inman Hunter
   ISBN 185532 203
Land Rover: A Tough Fifty Years, Chris Bennett & Nick Dimbleby
   ISBN 185532 641 8
VW Beetle: Restorotion, Preparation, Maintenance, Jim Tyler
   ISBN 185532 359 1
Mercedes-Benz SL & SLC, L.J.K. Setright
   ISBN 185532 880 1

For a catalogue of all books by Osprey Military, Aviation and Automotive
please write to:

The Marketing Manager, Osprey Publishing Ltd.,
P.O. Box 140, Wellingborough, Northants NN8 4ZA
United Kingdom

Or visit our website: http://www.osprey-publishing.co.uk

Contents

Introduction

The story behind the Volkswagen Beetle is one of the most dramatic in the entire world of motoring. Thought up in the depressive 1930s as an economy car by the celebrated initiator of the fabulous Auto Union Grand Prix racing cars, Dr. Ferdinand Porsche, the idea was taken on by no less a person than Adolf Hitler. Hitler first backed the Beetle as a car for which the workers of Germany could subscribe (though in the event they never got them) and then made good use of the Volkswagen as war-transport.

Bombed by Allied aircraft, the VW factory at Wolfsburg was soon destroyed, only to rise from the rubble and ashes of destruction after it became apparent to the Allies that Germany needed work for her unemployed. During the postwar reparations Dr. Porsche's brilliant design was turned down by the Americans and British alike and the fine new factory devoted to its production was, at first, an ownerless and stateless concern. That notwithstanding, it was one of the most impressive and effective mass production factories in the world, creating Beetles at the rate of one every eight seconds.

Wolfsburg became an ideal workers' town, and the factory an unblemished showpiece. The Beetle itself was so unconventional, yet so well finished and influential, that it was hard to supress enthusiasm for it. It sold all over the globe in remarkable numbers, soon to be counted in millions. Now, decades later, the ubiquitous Beetle is still not quite dead. This is its story in words and pictures.

I suppose I should not be surprised at having been asked to write this book, because I was such a keen and happy Beetle user in the mid-1950s that I could not resist warmly advocating the odd little car from the Black Forest. Indeed, I was so favourably disposed to the Beetle that I was frequently accused of being pro-German (on the contrary my father was killed during the First World War) and even of being in the pay of Wolfsburg!

I continued undeterred to enthuse in print about the air-cooled, rear-engined flat-four German car, because I believe that motoring writers should be beyond the influence of politics and National bias. Even now, when I am not at all sure that I would care to do much driving in a Beetle, because motoring standards change so quickly—daily travel in a VW Polo or a Golf though would be something else—I am apt to be hailed as the Beetle-man. Some years ago, when Cliff Michelmore interviewed me at my home in Wales for the BBC, he began by asking me if I were not ashamed of being so much in favour of German cars and of giving foreign products such a boost; his 'homework' was a bit dated, but as I have said, the Beetle image has stuck. I expect this was why a former *Daily Express* news sub-editor called Bob Wyse called on me in 1960 to ask whether I thought there was room for one more motoring magazine, providing it was devoted to the Volkswagen. And why, when it thought in 1977 that the end of Beetle production was in sight *The Guardian* turned to me to write the obituary.

By the time the war was over the Volkswagens were on sale all over the world, the British concessionaires operated from these plush showrooms at Lord's Court, in London's St. John's Wood Road, with a service station with waiting room behind them. From the Beetle came all the other models

All of this stems from having believed without question in the Beetle, at a time when British family and economy cars were dull and out-dated. The 'Thing' from Wolfsburg bristled with ingenuity, those who used it were encouraged to think that the manufacturers and the British concessionaires were behind them to a man, and the VW spares service was as impeccable as any such complex operation ever can be. Which is why, when my wife and I were invited to the VW factory to see the millionth Beetle leave the long assembly line, I was proud to wave my VW ignition key in the air as we were jostled by even prouder workers, on that memorable occasion.

Which is, I suppose, why I have been picked on to write what follows. . . .

Chapter 1
In the beginning

The Volkswagen Beetle that was to make such an impact on the automotive world and reach record mass-production output figures soon after the end of the Second World War had quite modest beginnings. By the nineteen-thirties the need for smaller, less-expensive, and more economical cars was recognized the World over. In Germany as much as in other parts of Europe, the economic depression was spreading rapidly from America, and motoring, already accepted as one of man's more enjoyable pursuits, and the motor-car his most desirable possession after his women and a place to reside in, was under fire in terms of its continuing viability with the masses.

It so happened that this monetary chill-wind coincided with the celebrated engineer Professor Ferdinand Porsche having set up his own designing and consultancy office in Stuttgart. Dr. Porsche was by then a very famous automobile creator. As has oft been told, he had been responsible for some very notable motor-cars, even prior to the outbreak of the Kaiser War. For example, he began with the electric Lohner-Porsche Chaise of 1900, and produced other electric vehicles for the Viennese company. Porsche then moved to the Austro-Daimler Company whose cars then became popular with some of the European Royalty. Increased in power, one of Porsche's designs the 28/32 hp Austro-Daimler 'Maja' of 1909 performed impressively in the

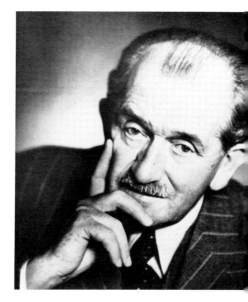

Professor Ferdinand Porsche—designer of the VW Beetle

Prince Henry Trial of that year. For the 1910 event Porsche produced a team of cars that was to establish a landmark in motoring history. Fitted with tulip-shaped touring bodywork, these 86 bhp or so Austro-Daimlers were capable of a timed speed of 87 mph, some ten mph quicker than the best of their rivals. Porsche won the 1910 Prince Henry Trials outright, with his team mates, if one can so-call Fischer and Count Schonfeld, following him into second and third places.

Porsche designed other, smaller, Austro-Daimler fast touring cars (some of which were used in competition), which William Beardmore imported into England, Malcolm Campbell being interested, and he was responsible for the Austro-Daimler aero-engines, also imported by Beardmore. This led to him becoming Technical Director of Daimler-Motoren AG in 1923—which became the Daimler-Benz Company in 1926; need one say more? It was then that Ferdinand Porsche, who was later to plan economy cars destined to develop into the immortal Volkswagen Beetle, did some of this greatest work. He designed the leading Mercedes racing cars, as well as the production models, and just before he severed his connection with the influential German Company, Porsche had laid out the plans for those fabulous supercharged 33/180, 36/220, and 38/250 Mercedes-Benz sports-cars unquestionably Teutonic, and so impressive when the blowers came in as their accelerators were fully depressed to provide maximum urge for accelerating. They were to have many wins to their credit, including Caracciola's victory in the 1929 Ulster TT.

It is ironical that the dominance of the newly-elected Benz directors at Stuttgart was the cause of Dr. Porsche's leaving the company, as some years later he was to be fully responsible for the

The ubiquitous VW Beetle has often been compared with that other immortal people's car, the Model T Ford, of which more than 15 million were produced between 1907 and 1926, an output surpassed by the Beetle. At first Henry Ford announced that the Model T could be had in any colour so long as it was black. For this reason the author specified a black Beetle when he used the VW product

first of the revolutionary Auto-Union Grand Prix racing cars (rear-engined, like the Volkswagen Beetle), which were in 1936 to trounce the might of the Mercedes-Benz racing department under the experienced Herr Alfred Neubauer, the cars competing under the three-pointed star of Stuttgart not getting back into their stride until 1937.

From Mercedes, Porsche went to the Steyr-Werke AG in Austria, after turning down an offer to work for Skoda in Czechoslovakia, for although he had been born in the German area of that country he was unable to converse in the Czech language. In Austria Porsche further enhanced his engineering reputation by designing some advanced models for Steyr, including the straight-eight Steyr 'Austria' with independent rear suspension. Seeing difficulties ahead, as a merger between Steyr and Austro-Daimler would have led to a recurrence of the clashes experienced when he was with the latter company, he resigned and went back to Stuttgart to set up the afore-mentioned Consultancy. Almost immediately Wanderer commissioned a design from Dr. Porsche: this 2-litre overhead-valve six with its light-alloy cylinder block and swing-axle rear suspension was a great success.

The organization that Porsche set up was no hole-in-the-corner affair. He took accommodation at Kronenstrasse 24, in Stuttgart, and employed a talented staff. Karl Rabe, earlier Porsche's assistant at Austro-Daimler, who had risen to the position of Chief Designer at Steyr-Daimler-Puch, was the first to join, and other who came to work for Porsche included Joseph Kales an expert in air-cooled engines, notably those used in Tatra cars, and the designers Fröhlich and Zahradnick, while Adolf Rosenberger, an amateur racing driver who had found it difficult to obtain a place in a German team at this time because he was a

Ugly is only skin-deep.

It may not be much to look at. But beneath that humble exterior beats an air-cooled engine. It won't boil over and ruin your piston rings. It won't freeze over and ruin your life. It's in the back of the car, where the weight on the rear wheels makes the traction very good in snow and sand. And it will give you about 29 miles to a gallon of gas.

After a while you get to like so much about the VW, you even get to like what it looks like.

You find that there's enough legroom for almost anybody's legs. Enough headroom for almost anybody's head. With a hat on it. Snug-fitting bucket seats. Doors that close so well you can hardly close them. (They're so airtight, it's better to open the window a crack first.)

Those plain, unglamorous wheels are each suspended independently. So when a bump makes one wheel bounce, the bounce doesn't make the other wheel bump. It's things like that you pay the $1663* for, when

you buy a VW. The ugliness doesn't add a thing to the cost of the car.

That's the beauty of it.

©Volkswagen of America, Inc. *Suggested Retail Price, West Coast P.O.E., Local Taxes and Other Dealer Delivery Charges, If Any, Additional.

Jew, looked after administration. Others who joined at this early stage were Mickl, a mathematician, Komenda, a specialist in body design, and in September 1934, designer Reimspiess. And there was Ferdinand's son Ferry, who was to have such a profound influence after the war, as the creator of the Porsche sports coupés; (but that is a story best told by the late Denis Jenkinson).

Getting to grips with his desire to design a small economy, or people's car, Porsche began to consider the various technical permutations available. From the design of powerful, lorry-like Mercedes-Benz sports cars he was now turning to a car that was supposed to be built in millions. Moreover, it was the Doctor's intention that this should be a world car in its adaptability to cold and hot climates alike, tough, essentially reliable and and in fact a spiritual successor to the Model T Ford, of which 15,007,033 had been made in the period 1908 to 1927, before the competition caught up with Henry Ford and he moved on.

Ferdinand Porsche had become accustomed to living well, when he had been toiling for Austro-Daimler and Daimler-Benz. From coming to Vienna as a penniless immigrant he had prospered, and could afford a fine house, a motor yacht, and the upbringing of two children, son Ferry and a daughter, by the age 56. Yet he was quite capable of thinking in terms of any kind of motor vehicle or internal-combustion engine that was currently required and it was now that he shelved ideas for luxury models, like his still-born 3.2-litre eight-cylinder streamlined Wanderer and the Steyr 'Austria', and those fast Mercedes-Benz, and prepared to concentrate on a vehicle for the masses who found freedom and a new pleasure in personal ownership of a motor-car.

Before his resignation from Daimler-Benz in

The front aspect of the Beetle gave excellent driver-visibility but when the hood (or bonnet) was lifted there was no engine—only a cavity for luggage and the big fuel tank. This picture was used with one of VW's famous advertisement layouts, captioned 'Ugly is only skin-deep'

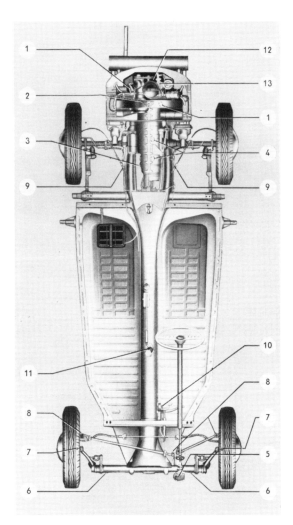

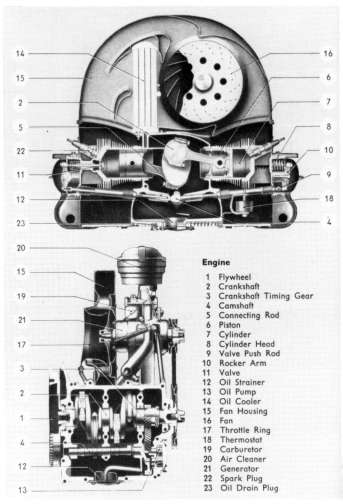

Engine

1 Flywheel
2 Crankshaft
3 Crankshaft Timing Gear
4 Camshaft
5 Connecting Rod
6 Piston
7 Cylinder
8 Cylinder Head
9 Valve Push Rod
10 Rocker Arm
11 Valve
12 Oil Strainer
13 Oil Pump
14 Oil Cooler
15 Fan Housing
16 Fan
17 Throttle Ring
18 Thermostat
19 Carburetor
20 Air Cleaner
21 Generator
22 Spark Plug
23 Oil Drain Plug

This picture, taken from the splendidly-illustrated Beetle handbook, shows well the ingenious layout of the insect. Note the platform-chassis with central backbone, through which ran the control rods and cables, the trailing-arm all-round independent suspension, and rear-located battery

The durable air-cooled 'boxer' engine of the VW Beetle is dissected here for the benefit of engineers

October 1928, after he had set his seal on the great Mercedes-Benz sports-cars but before he had seen their full fruition, in the guise of the SSK and SSKL models, Porsche had wanted to produce a really small motor-car of around one-litre in engine size. However, he met opposition from the newly-arrived directors from the Benz branch of Mercedes-Benz and the project was dropped. Daimler-Benz have never really exploited the smallest of cars, although there had been the water-cooled rear-engined 1.3-litre Type 130H Mercedes-Benz of 1933, during the reign of Hans Nibel, and its more powerful derivative, the Type 170H.

Porsche was inclined from the start to favour air-cooling, if only to humour those who had to run their personal transport in terms of very hot or very cold weather and, moreover, might be careless or mistrustful of anti-freeze solutions. He had a good precedent in the air-cooled aero-engine he had designed for Austro-Daimler as far back as 1912. But Porsche was a thinking, cautious engineer and he put many plans and designs on paper before deciding on the final shape of his economy car. At the time when he was embarking on the genesis of the Volkswagen Beetle idea, Ferdinand Porsche had other projects to think about as well. It would appear that he began planning this little car in 1930 but that it was not until late in September 1931 that he was finally satisfied with the car's definitive form, and could discuss it in some detail with his staff.

Chapter 2
Prewar small-car engineering

At this time the small car was in common use throughout Europe and even true miniatures of the baby-car catagory had been accepted by the car-buying public. The crude 'stick-and-string' cyclecars had had an unexpectedly large following for a while, from 1912 until the early nineteen-twenties, when more conventional cars such as the Rover Eight and similar 'half-and-half' developments had undermined the cyclecar regime. By 'half-and-half' I mean those chassis which still made use of an air-cooled power-pack of the greatest simplicity but had 'big-car' type gearboxes and transmissions. The successful Rover Eight, for instance, used a flat-twin, that is to say horizontally-opposed two-cylinder engine (its protruding cylinders are said to have glowed cherry-red at night when the car was grinding up long hills!), cooled by direct air-flow.

Such cars, selling at under £200 in Britain, were preferable to cruder belt or chain-driven machines, unless these were especially cheap to purchase. There was still, it is true, quite a following for the ultra-simple three-wheeler, led by the pioneering Morgan from Malvern, but reduced taxation rates and low first cost were the clue to their continuing popularity, and in time Morgan, BSA, and other makes of three-wheeler went over to water-cooled four-cylinder engines. At this time of economy-car proliferation, odd designs would be encountered, like the four-cylinder, two-stroke Trojan, with connecting rods that bent intentionally as the engine with its paired cylinders revolved. This one had a two-speed epicyclic transmission like the Model-T Ford and final drive to one of its two rear wheels by duplex chain. Early models had overlapping cantiliver springs, and thus ran comfortably on solid tyres. This sort of thing, the Trojan being advertised as less expensive than walking, and friction-drive small-cars such as the Unit No. 1 and the GWK, were not throwbacks to the cyclecar age but more direct replacements at the bottom end of the market.

All this virtually ended with advent of the Austin Seven in 1922, a true baby based on big-car specifications, with three forward speeds, four-wheel-brakes, and in time an electric starter (it had had dynamo lighting from its inception). The now legendary Austin 7 not only saved Sir Herbert Austin's financial bacon, it set a fresh fashion in tiny but essentially practical motor-transport for the millions—'Motoring at Tram Fare', in fact. It quickly killed off the cyclecar, most of the three-wheelers, and heavier motorcycle-combinations. It used a four-cylinder water-cooled side-valve engine of 747 cc. The Austin 7 had its counterpart in France in the 4CV and 5CV Peugeot and the 5CV Citröen. Both had similar water-cooled four-pot power plants front-mounted in the classical idiom. Porsche was in favour of putting the engine at the back of the vehicle, a layout used for a few minimal vehicles in the £100-car bracket, and for the Benz *Tropfen-wagen* racing car and Rumpler saloon in Germany: this last was a big luxury machine. Porsche also favoured opposed cylinders, which the new generation of babies, the overhead camshaft Singer Junior, and new Morris Minor and the Triumph Super Seven with a three-bearing crankshaft in its side-valve engine, rejected in favour of normal in-line four-cylinder engines. Of the really successful makes, only Jowett up in Yorkshire favoured a flat-twin, and that was invariably water-cooled. Later, indeed, the Jowett brothers were to introduce a horizontally-opposed *four-*cylinder car.

Most of this may have been unknown or if known, unlikely to influence Dr. Porsche, working away at his new economy-car project in Germany. He must have been aware of the minimal Hanomag with its single cylinder, and of the more conventional Opel 4/12PS 'Laubfrosch', suggesting 'tree frog', dating from 1924, and of the 3/15PS BMW-Dixi a licence produced Austin Seven, introduced in 1927. Also in Germany was the little DKW twin-cylinder two-stroke car using front-wheel-drive, after that factory's spell with rear-wheel-drive models. In its case the cylinders were a vertical pair, set across the chassis frame, a layout made famous by Sir Alec Issigonis' great BMC Mini Minor after the war. But if he was aware of these various permutations of the economy-car technique, Porsche would have none of it. He used a clean sheet of paper on his drawing board, when planning the car that was to emerge as the Beetle.

It wasn't only the engine, its cylinder formation and method of cooling, that was to be 'different' in Porsche's design, for what he now called his new Project 12. (Earlier designs from his Consultancy Studio had been consecutively numbered.) He studied a new concept of road-wheel suspension, and after employing leaf springs for the earlier Zundapp prototypes, Porsche came up with the torsion-bar as giving the

springing effects required, with very little in-
trusion on the space available, which is always a
criterion in small cars. Torsion-bar suspension for
touring cars dated from its employment by
the Welsh racing-driver/designer J. G. Parry
Thomas, who introduced it, with anti-roll bars for
good measure, on his Leyland Eight luxury-car
chassis of 1920, and which he used so very
effectively on his Leyland-Thomas racing cars at
Brooklands Track from 1922 until 1926.

The story goes that Porsche wanted the final
design for Project 12 to be completed within three
months, by his team of skilled draughtsmen
working at their nine drawing boards, after which
would come consideration as to how a prototype
could be built for road testing. It is immediately

The beginnings of the Beetle can be traced to this Type 12 Ferdinand Porsche-designed small-car built in the Zundapp factory in Nürnberg in 1932

The Type 12 was followed by the Type 32, constructed by NSU at Neckarsulm in 1933/34

interesting that the first prototype bore a very close resemblance to the now well-known VW Beetle. For example, the air-cooled engine was positioned at the back, the body was a two-door saloon of decidedly 'insect' aspect, and it is noteworthy that even the spare wheel was mounted in the enclosed front luggage compartment. Moreover, all four wheels were independently sprung, by torsion-bars. The difference lay in Porsche's experimental engine, which was a five-cylinder radial, intended to give 26 bhp at 3200 rpm. Radial engines were not unknown for motor-car installation, but they were decidedly unusual. In earlier days the CAR, a Roy Fedden design from Bristol, had used a three-cylinder unit of this type, and at about the same period the Enfield-Allday had had a five-cylinder radial engine. In 1923 the North-Lucas 1½-litre stream-lined saloon had a rear-mounted air-cooled 5-cylinder radial engine. In France the Lafitte used

A rare photograph of the first experimental VW engine, the Doppelkolben motor, with paired pistons and side-mounted cooling fan. It was made in two capacities, 850 cc for the Model A and 1000 cc for the Model A1

a three-cylinder air-cooled radial engine, pivoted to engage the friction disc of its transmission system, and after the war the stillborn Kendall people's car, planned for production at Grantham in England, had such an engine at the rear.

The prototype Porsche was quite small, its wheelbase being 2500 mm or close to 8 ft 3 in, with a four-foot wheel track, and the dry weight was quoted as 900 kg or 1984 lb. The question of getting any German car manufacturer interested in it at this time of world recession was a real problem. Fortunately for Porsche's peace of mind, the motorcycle industry heard of it and showed some enthusiasm. It was to Dr. Fritz Neumeyer of the Zundapp Company at Nuremberg that Porsche took his drawings. The outcome was fruitful, inasmuch as Zundapp agreed to reimburse him for some of the expenses already incurred and to build three prototype cars, but with five-cylinder *water-cooled* radial engines. Production of these and their bodies (by Reutter) proceeded in secrecy. By 1932 the first cars were being tested, but without much initial success, and it wasn't long before Zundapp lost interest. History relates that, as agreed, Porsche kept the first of these prototypes and used it continually until it was destroyed by a war-time bomb on his Stuttgart garage in 1944, the other two Zundapp-Porsches going the same way, during an air-raid on Nuremberg. Wilhelm von Opel has been blamed for pouring cold water on the project, to safeguard his own small cars.

Chapter 3
The Beetle is born

Things were now moving in a sinister direction in peacetime Germany. Whether or not Dr. Porsche had inklings of what lay ahead, or of how Herr Hitler would use International motor-racing as a propaganda tool for his Nazi Party, is not known. The fact is that, after being invited to Russia but returning quickly to his design office in Stuttgart, he discussed the advantages of having the plans for a racing-car ready should the German Industry ever require one. For this purpose he set up a separate concern, a High Performance Vehicle Company, which was later to design the very exciting rear-engined Grand Prix Auto Unions, pitted against the Mercedes-Benz racers in a Hitlerian dream of German automotive domination. It was as this other, very different, project got under way that another attempt was made to get the Porsche small car into production. This time NSU was approached, with excellent results. Their Herr von Falkenhayn agreed to stand the costs of making three prototypes and now Porsche got his way, which was to change the water-cooled five-cylinder radial engine for an air-cooled flat-four, cooled by a belt-driven fan and using push-rod-operated overhead valves—a step closer, indeed very close, to the Volkswagen as we all know it! It has been suggested that an Englishman who had worked at the Norton motorcycle factory was responsible for this horizontally-opposed engine. But although, as a good reporter, I spent some time in 1956 investigating this, I got no further. The story, since denied, is that Walter William Moore, who went to NSU and there designed such successful engines as the parallel-twin supercharged racing unit used in their TT and GP machines, conceived the VW before Porsche absorbed the drawings.

Be that as it may, this was a time when the paths of Porsche and Hitler were converging. Hitler had told Auto Union of his desire that they should race on the world's circuits, and it was their intention to use Porsche's designs if anything came of this. Hitler had also pontificated at the

Why, from an early stage, the Porsche innovatory small-car earned the 'Beetle' appellation!

1933 Berlin Motor Show about the pleasures the population of Germany, of which he had been elected Chancellor, and Leader of the National Social Democratic Party, could enjoy if a really inexpensive people's car were available to them. Porsche was driven to Berlin in his 3.8-litre Wanderer to meet the Auto Union directors, and he discovered that Hitler was there as well. It is said that it was Porsche who convinced the German Dictator that he would need Auto Union as well as Mercedes-Benz if the might of technical Germany was to be apparent on the race-tracks. I refer to this to indicate how Hitler became aware of Porsche and his accomplishments at this time,

This was one of the test-bed V1/V2 chassis, in which experimental VW engines were installed. It had a wooden floor and was devoid of shock-absorbers

By 1936 Daimler-Benz had been instructed to build Porsche's experimental cars, in the Mercedes factory. This is a rather surprising cabriolet version, retaining the small front-boot lid opened with a knurled knob, but definitely shaping the way to the ultimate Beetle

although then it was apparently only motor-racing that was discussed.

Meanwhile, the three prototype NSU vehicles had been built and tested. But this project became as redundant as the Zundapp one when Fiat held NSU to an existing agreement for making their cars at Heilbronn, leaving NSU to concentrate in the remaining pre-war years on their motorcycles. The Porsche design office then concentrated on getting the bugs out of the Auto Union racing car. Until, that is, the next summons to meet Herr Hitler. This time it was not the heady subject of motor-racing but his People's Car dream that the German Chancellor discussed.

Hitler knew more about cars than might have

been imagined, and he now outlined his requirements to the great engineer seated before him.
The Volks Wagen was to be a simple vehicle, able
to accommodate the parents and three children if
needs be—pure-bred children of course—and a
little luggage. It must be cheap to maintain and to
repair, able to run without stress along the new
German motor roads, the *Autobahnen* of which
Herr Hitler was so proud, return some 40 mpg, and
cost less than 1000 marks, say £50.

This was something that Dr. Porsche realized
would be next-to-impossible to achieve. In England there had been inexpensive cars for the
masses, for those indulging in what was sometimes called The New Motoring. William Morris

*Ferry Porsche, Prof.
Porsche's son who was so
closely associated with the
later Porsche sports cars,
driving one of the early VW
cabriolet Beetles. Note the
centrally-mounted horn-grille
and his lady friend's
typically-German white linen
flying helmet*

had produced a £100 Morris Minor in 1931, a simple two-seater sold for this low price by denuding it of all essential equipment and giving it a dark grey paint job, with unplated headlamps, etc. Ford broke into this preserve with the first £100 saloon a few years later. Otherwise, even the target of £100 or less had been confined to terribly crude cyclecars, or to unconventional or small-output cars, such as the rear-engined two-cylinder Waverley, the two-stroke Seaton-Petter and the conventional four-cylinder Gillett, all of which soon faded away. All three were 1927 manifestations.

However, the requirements of Herr Hitler were not to be lightly ignored, so Porsche dusted off his drawings. There were many problems to face. When the official contract was received it was seen that the price of each car had dropped to 900 marks, which was in no way to be exceeded, for a run of 50,000 VWs; and this on a budget of scarcely £10,000 (200,000 marks) for the development of three prototypes. Moreover, all this time Porsche was very busy with the Auto Union racing cars, which had already attained sensational speeds in initial record-bid appearances and had won the German Grand Prix, one of them, driven by Hans von Stuck, trouncing the fabulous new team of Mercedes-Benz.

To his new assignment for Hitler, Porsche gave the designation Volkswagen Series 3. It involved getting out three prototypes of the new small People's Car within a space of ten months. Hitler had decided that the German Automobile Industry would sign this contract, not the German Government. To keep the cost down, Hitler had foreseen that component parts must be supplied by the German Motor Industry. This, for a start, angered Herr von Opel, who himself had an interest in economy cars. Nevertheless, Porsche

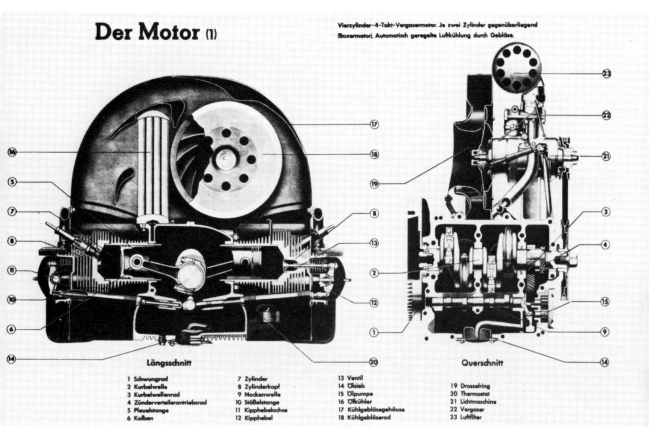

Der Motor (1)

Vierzylinder-4-Takt-Vergasermotor. Je zwei Zylinder gegenüberliegend (Boxermotor). Automatisch geregelte Luftkühlung durch Gebläse.

Längsschnitt

Querschnitt

1 Schwungrad	7 Zylinder	13 Ventil	19 Drosselring
2 Kurbelwelle	8 Zylinderkopf	14 Ölsieb	20 Thermostat
3 Kurbelwellenrad	9 Nockenwelle	15 Ölpumpe	21 Lichtmaschine
4 Zündverteilerantriebsrad	10 Stößelstange	16 Ölkühler	22 Vergaser
5 Pleuelstange	11 Kipphebelachse	17 Kühlgebläsegehäuse	23 Luftfilter
6 Kolben	12 Kipphebel	18 Kühlgebläserad	

built his prototypes, using the platform chassis, steel body, and torsion-bar suspension he regarded as the most economical method of proceeding, but still undecided on the final form of engine. In the end, a flat-four or 'boxer-motor', with four air-cooled cylinders, was used. It had overhead valves, and a capacity of 985 cc. The three experimental Volks were subjected to very tough high mileage testing, teams of drivers thrashing the tiny Beetles day and night, without showing them any mercy. The Motor Industry was prevailed upon to conduct its own critical and intensive examinations of the vehicle. This en-

Engine of the later experimental and first production Beetles. Those who understand German have a key to the mechanical components!

Taking final form. Two Type 30 Beetles of circa 1937, the earlier one on the right

abled the criticisms of Porsche's design to be made to Hitler, via the German Secretary of State, without pouring cold water on a scheme so close to the Hitlerian heart. It must have been very difficult for Opel, about to launch the first of their low-priced Kadett saloons, a lively car with Dubonnet independent-front-suspension. This one, although alleged to be constructed of pressed cardboard and tin (as was the DKW Meister-klasse) by snide commentators, sold in Britain just before the war for £135 and was used by many well-known motoring personalities, who found its 60 mph cruising pace and good fuel economy to their liking. Objections were raised, it is said, notably by Herr Opel.

However, Hitler would have none of it, and in his speech made at the opening of the 1937 Berlin Motor Show he announced that the State-produced Volkswagen would go into production. It has to be conceded that Hitler and his Nazi Party had done a great deal to encourage motoring. The great new Autobahnen had been constructed, linking German cities as never before in the realms of road transportation. Motor tax had been cut in Germany, to encourage the purchase of more new cars. Motor racing was seen as a Nazi publicity campaign, and now Hitler was proposing to build a great new factory to be devoted entirely to the production, in enormous numbers, of a car for his people. They could buy stamps towards purchase of these new Volks Autos, in the same way as we can now save for a TV licence.

Whether Hitler was sincere, or whether the whole plan was a vast con-trick aimed at securing a plentiful supply of small but rugged military vehicles with which to conduct his war in Europe, must be left to conjecture, or to the social historians. The fact is that Porsche received a

An early example of the Series 3 VW Beetle

31

There was not much outward difference between the Type 60 Beetle of 1935/36, and the earlier models

mandate for military VWs alongside the civilian model, and the saving-stamp scheme went ahead causing, it is said, more than 336,000 German citizens to lose some 280,000,000 marks in a lost dream! The money collected was lodged in an East German bank and was legitimately seized by the Russians as war reparations, after the hostilities ceased. That is to anticipate, however.

In the 1936/37 period Porsche went to America, not only to see his V16 Auto Union beat the field at the Roosevelt Speedway, but to study the successful mass-production of automobiles at Ford and other plants. On his return, testing of experimental Volkswagens was speeded up, now that it was known that Hitler had ensured that the necessary finance had been guaranteed by the German Labour Organization, under Robert Ley.

Thirty cars of a specification closer to the envisaged production model were made by Mercedes-Benz, under their then Director Herr Kissel (Jakob Werlin soon succeeded him), for although the task was distasteful to him he had little option when the order came from Herr Werlin, close friend and motor industry advisor to Hitler. These later prototypes were known as the Series-30 Volkswagen, and they were to be tested over a distance of $2\frac{1}{2}$ million kilometres, in a matter of three or four months. The die was indeed cast! Porsche's staff of around 80 had transferred all the required alterations to detail drawings, and Hitler agreed to 200 Nazi Stormtroopers testing the vehicles, operating from a military base at Kornwestheim near Stuttgart. The unenviable task of over-seeing this gigantic test

If the VW Beetle of 1936 looked like a rather poor model-maker's version of what we were to know later as the famous postwar model, all the features are already there—rear-louvred bonnet, the plain wheel knave-plates, the two doors, and the pronounced mudguards, forming the famous beetle profile

A VW Beetle coming off the production-line at the Mercedes-Benz factory in Stuttgart in 1937. Note the inbuilt headlamps, and the luggage boot ready for later extension downwards to the car's nose

programme fell to Porsche's son Ferry. It is said that never before had any motor vehicle been so exhaustively tested or so much detailed technical data recorded for the Series 3 vehicles, and this may well remain true even of post-war cars from the biggest automotive plants, for not only were more than $1\frac{1}{2}$ million test miles covered, but laboratory records were made of all aspects of the little vehicles. Moreover, having caned the first batch of thirty Daimler-Benz made cars as hard as possible, similar tests to destruction were carried out on a further thirty prototypes, called the Type-60, Series 38 Volkswagens.

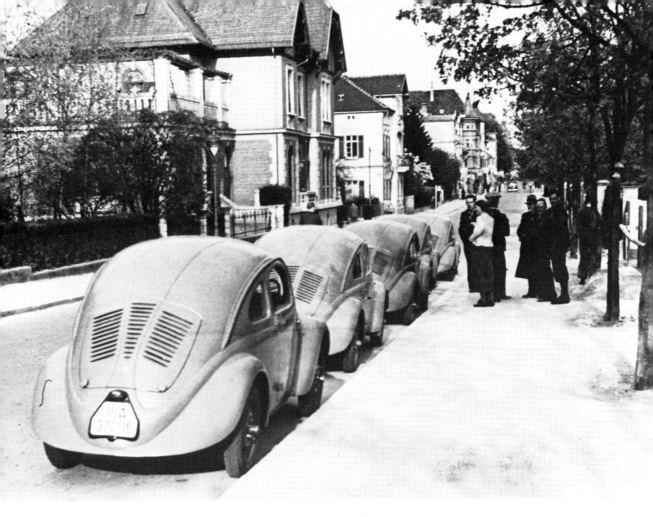

When the testing had been completed and the Volkswagen was ready for production, there remained the problem of where it could be assembled, ready for those then-seemingly lucky German workers and other citizens to take delivery. Herr Hitler's arrogance was never better emphasized than in his People's Car concept. He had indeed grandiose ideas about it, specifying that initial production of VWs should be at the rate of about 400,000 cars to 500,000 cars a year, leading on to a million per annum. Think of it, some 83,000 VWs a month, or 2700 every working day, of a brand-new design, in a factory

Arousing interest—a line-up of VW Beetles, circa 1937. No doubt test runs were in progress

An interesting picture showing a VW being assembled at the Mercedes-Benz factory. From the operative's expression it appears to have been a top-secret operation!

not yet built, or a site chosen for it! The good that might have arisen from this was that about 18,000 people would find employment in the 'Strength-through-Joy' motor-works, with something like 30,000 being needed eventually. To obtain the real experts among production engineers, however, Porsche was prevailed upon to look for such talent among German technicians who had emigrated to America, on his visits there, persuade them to return to the now-Hitlerized Fatherland and work in the cause of the people's car.

Procuring a site for a factory able to cope with such a volume of production was now imperative to Hitler. A dramatic sub-plot had been woven around this particular aspect of the Volkswagen Beetle. Maps of Germany were apparently studied, to no avail. Low-flying military aeroplanes were brought in, from which Dr. Bodo Lafferentz (who had been ordered by Robert Ley to find a piece of land some twenty square miles, adjacent to railway and canal facilities, where the VW could be built and a new town developed to house those who would make it) frantically scanned the terrain below. Soon the search was concentrated on a location by the railway line from the Ruhr, between Hanover and Berlin, a plain with a canal passing through it. The whole project, the search included, was top-secret. But secrets have a habit of leaking out and when Count von Schulenberg was told of trespassers on his estate surrounding the 14th-century Schloss Wolfsburg, it wasn't long before he was aware of what was afoot. He

Another view of the pre-war Type 60 VW Beetle, this one dating from 1937

set up strenuous plans to stop the conversion of a fine area of farming and hunting country into a vast new motor-factory. To no avail, of course. Big Mercedes-Benz and Horch saloons, pennants flying from their radiator caps would appear in the region, while the land was surveyed and assessed. And that is how Wolfsburg became the home of Volkswagen and all the drama and intrigue that was to follow. . . .

It is a measure of the power Hitler already had and the fear he could instill that the the Count and Countess von Schulenberg could get no help from old friends among high-ranking Army officers, nor from a boyhood friend who was then Minister of the German Land Department, nor from the the Ministry of Forestry. They were quite helpless. The fine estate the Count's family had occupied for over 500 years, with its ancient oak tress, sooned to be felled in their thousands, was at the mercy of Hitler. And obviously no mercy would be shown, now that Ley had been informed by Lafferentz that a suitable sight for the VW factory had been found. When Hitler opened the Berlin Motor Show of 1938 a model of the proposed new motor-town of Wolfsburg was exhibited there. To this day Wolfsburg Castle is used as a trademark by VW.

It is even said that as a last resort the unfortunate Count von Schulenberg used the excuse of plagues of gnats invading his estate, but of course, this was to no avail. The next need was for a skilled and experienced architect to design the great city of Wolfsburg. The celebrated Albert Speer might well have been given the task, except that Hitler kept him busy on a new Nazi project for Greater Berlin. He was ear-marked as adviser to the Wolfsburg plans, but the man actually responsible was Herr Koller, at the time Town Engineer at Augsbug, in Southern Germany. Jakob Werlin insisted on his being employed and apparently his big black Mercedes-Benz limousine took Werlin to the historic town, to procure Koller's services. This Austrian who had gone to Vienna University, completing his studies in Berlin, was the architect of the new Wolfsburg project, his plans accepted in the face of those specially prepared by the learned staff of Brunswick University.

Most of the tools for making the forthcoming VW were of German origin, but the sort of mass-production machinery that only the USA could provide was paid for by money that the cunning Herr Werlin was able to extract from the tight purse-strings of Hermann Göring, who controlled Government spending. Another obstacle overcome!

Chapter 4
A factory for the Beetle

So, while the final 985 cc Volkswagens were reaching the end of the strenuous test programme, and Dr. Porsche was about ready to release the production version of the Beetle, which came to be known as the Series 38, the plans for the factory were being pushed through by Peter Koller with all possible speed, attainable only perhaps in Hitler's Germany. The laying of the foundation-stone was, predictably an enormous piece of Nazi propaganda. Hitler had

Nearing pre-war finality. This is actually a wooden mock-up of the VW body, for the Reutter coachbuilders to work to. Note that the doors are by now front-hinged and the bonnet or front boot-lid is extended to meet the front valance

Top *This picture is interesting, as showing the oldest VW Beetle in existence, No. 13 of the production series, now in a German museum*

Left *A handout picture of the left-hand-drive 1938 Type 60 KdF, so-called limousine. It would have looked better with the wheel knave-plates in place, but as the German subscribers never got one, perhaps it didn't really matter . . .*

Hitlerian propaganda! Eight VW Beetles lined-up for a public viewing in Berlin a year before the war. Note that now four of them have the fold-back sun-roof. The cars on the far side of the road are rather interesting, too. The German workers had been giving five DM a week towards these VWs they never received and when this picture was released there were said to be 169,741 of them

Right *A tantalising sight. The Beetle on show at the 1939 Berlin Motor Cycle and Car Exhibition, apparently being guarded by the SS*

Below *Before the bombing. A line-up of completed VW Beetles under the sign of the Swastika, to celebrate Prof. Porsche's birthday*

DIE ERSTEN IM VOLKSWAGENWERK HERGESTELLTEN KDF-WAGEN

Zum 66. Geburtstage unseres Betriebsführers Herrn Prof. Dr. ing. h.c.F. Porsche

made pointed reference to his People's Car project at a speech he made on 18 February 1938, when he opened the 28th International Berlin Automobile and Motor-Cycle Exhibition. Incidentally, journalists from other countries were encouraged to visit these exhibitions, with the temptation of free tickets and free air travel to Berlin if the request was made through German Embassies.

A 1942 Beetle photographed in Wolfsburg in 1977, showing the small split rear window of those early models

45

The VW design of the brilliant Prof. Porsche was quickly adapted to the requirements of war, and the German Panzer-Divisions' need to be fully mobile. This is the Type 82 Kübelwagen

After the war I asked the PRO of Mercedes-Benz why the Mercedes company had held Laurence Pomeroy, Jnr, in such high esteem when he was a very young man. 'Ah', I was told, 'he may then have been comparatively unknown, although the son of a great engineer, but now, you see, he is Technical Editor of *Motor* and a good friend of ours; we could not forsee that this might come about, but as a safeguard, we offered him hospitality, back in 1938.' The Volkswagen was possibly receiving similar encouragement from those who showed any interest in it!

Hitler in his speech, had said that the four-year development programme of the Volkswagen had paid off, and was nearly at an end. The car would be produced at a price everyone would be able to afford, in the most modern plant in the world.

The foundation stone at Wolfsburg was laid with immense pomp and ceremony, on 26 May 1938. Hitler told the assembled multitudes that here was a car to bring them joy, created by the power of Nazi Germany to sell for less than the equivalent of £50. It would be called the KdF— 'Strength-through-Joy'. It was a clever trick to take the Nation's mind off the Austrian *Anschluss* and the impending invasion of Czechoslovakia.

That did not stop work proceeding apace on the VW factory. Using conscripted labour, some of it marshalled from Italy's unemployed on the orders

Purposeful cross-country vehicle. It is not generally known that by 1942 the Beetle was given four-wheel-drive and extra-big track-grip tyres. The roller at the front was to help lift it over obstacles, and in this form it worked with the German Army up to 1945. Called the Type 87 Leichte Kavallerie model, the low gearing proved effective but limited top speed to under 40 mph

War-time fuel shortages called for radical modifications. This Beetle has been converted into a 'Holzbrenner', or wood-burner. The owner is refuelling it with wood chippings which, heated by a small stove under the hood, gave off 'producer gas' on which the engine could run, albeit with considerably reduced power

The rear-engine position of the VW lent itself to driving the propeller of this amphibian or Reitende Gebirgsmarine version, of which some 52,000 were built during the war

of Mussolini, the pace hotted up. At much the same time Porsche was ordered by the Fuhrer to design a military version of the Volkswagen, able to carry four soldiers and their equipment across difficult terrain. The hope for a People's Car was fading . . . . The German Army was essentially dependent on its highly mobile Panzer Divisions and it appears that the first military VWs emerged from the Wolfsburg factory early in 1940 to provide communication easily. As production increased, Rommel also made good use of those supplied to him and the *Kübelwagen* was found ideal for desert warfare. In other spheres of operation the amphibious, VW *Schwimmwagen* was just as successful.

Two war-time vehicles which have survived. The Beetle was found as a total wreck in Austria and the NSU motorcycle amphibian in a barn where it had rested for 22 years. Both are now running again

49

Chapter 5
End of the first phase, and a fresh start

When the tide of war turned against Germany, the Wolfsburg factory became an easy target for British and Allied bombers and it was nearly put out of action, although by no means destroyed structurally. What followed has all the qualities, if not of a fairy-tale, then of a cartoon or comic-opera, emphasizing that indeed truth is stranger than fiction.

While Dr' Porsche busied himself, albeit reluctantly, with the military version of the VW and went on to produce the amphibian model, using a four-bladed propeller driven by reduction gearing that also provided four-wheel-drive on land, the factory at Wolfsburg was only kept going by importing foreign slave labour, guarded by the German SS. Then Porsche's activities were directed away from his original concept, and he found himself designing tanks and similar weapons.

The bombing increased. An attacking enemy bomber, shot down by the anti-aircraft guns the Germans had installed to try to save the factory, fell on it, doing more damage, and by the time the war was almost in its last stages little production

was possible. Chaos soon broke out, with looting and street fighting. So it was decided that a three-man deputation should set out to look for the Occupation Forces and plead with them to take over the stricken town, which was apparently not on any military map and now deprived of all telephone communication. Legend has it, and I dare say it is correct, that the would-be rescue party of the Volkswagen factory, a Catholic priest, Antonius Wollingand, and the factory manager, Herr Brormann, drove away in the factory Doctor's car, as it displayed the sign of the Red Cross. Fortunately they encountered salvation near Fallersleben in the form of a small American military detachment led by a Lieutenant. With reluctance it was persuaded to drive on to Wolfsburg. From there the story takes on an improbable atmosphere. Reinforced, the Americans restored order in the rioting town. The British then took over, Wolfsburg falling within the British Zone of Western Germany. At first

A post-war picture outside the Wolfsburg Works, under British Military Government supervision

Top *Work gradually gets going again, at a slow pace, inside the badly-bombed VW factory; a scene from 1946*

Right *Assembly of Beetles in progress at the hastily-organised production-lines of the resuscitated factory in Wolfsburg*

The Ⓞ VOLKSWAGEN built during MARCH 1946 coming from Assembly Line

their task was to maintain law and order in the town, but eventually the British C.O. was asked by engineers if they could enter the derelict plant to see what could be saved. This led to Allied military vehicles being repaired, there, and by the autumn the REME moved in, Col. McEvoy, CBE putting in hand the resuscitation of the factory. From there it was only a matter of time before the Volkswagen was revived for British officers who knew of the merits of the military version and were only too glad to avail themselves of newly-built transport. Before the year was out over 700 VWs had been constructed.

It was then that the comic, or tragic, aspect emerged. The plant, stirring again, was a valuable

The pace soon quickened and cars began to roll off the assembly lines, to go into use for essential purposes. Here we can see the 1000th postwar Beetle coming out of the rebuilt factory

Top *It is 1947 and these brand-new Beetles have arrived in Holland; exports are starting!*

Right *Some of Heinz Nordhoff's know-how had come from visiting the Ford plants in America. Here Henry Ford II tries a VW in Köln in 1948*

Far right *It wasn't too long before a handsome cabriolet was added to the VW catalogue*

By 1949 Wolfsburg had its eyes on export markets and the finish of the Beetle was much enhanced by a fine paint job and chromium plating, while the body was made more accommodating and inviting within

war-prize, and should have been part of the victors' reparations scheme. But the American, French and Russian authorities were disinterested, and the same applied to the British. The British SMM & T visited the factory and arranged for experts, under Capt. J. S. Irving, designer of the 230 mph 'Golden Arrow' World's Land Speed Record car of 1929, to investigate. Perhaps influenced by worn-out military VW's, they pronounced the Porsche design a nonsense, and saw no future in it as a production proposition! The copiously illustrated report was based on an examination of a 1941 Type 82 military VW and

Stepping it up—production in full cry at Wolfsburg, with the complete welded-up body shells being dropped onto the unique Beetle chassis

57

Above *Impressive—although it is not far advanced into 1946, the front-axle and suspension line at Wolfsburg is obviously working to high-output capacity*

Above right *Cabriolet production, so this cannot be at Wolfsburg – the cabriolet was never built by VW. This is probably early production at Karmann of Osnabrück, the only 'official' Beetle Cabriolet builders, licenced from 1949. Not everyone in the UK was against the Beetle: Lt Col Guy Boas for one, argued that the acquisition of the plant would be "a splendid investment for this country, especially for overseas markets"*

was produced by the Rootes Group, led by the Engineering Department of Humber. It should be emphasized that at that time Rootes were pushing their own military vehicles with modified Super Snipe and Commer side-valve engines. That is how Volkswagen became, for many years, a great but ownerless motor-producing concern being neither State nor private property.

At that time the Occupation personnel had little option but to allow the factory to recuperate and flourish if only to avoid industrial and psychological deterioration within the conquered German nation. It also supplied badly needed vehicles to a car-famished Europe, vehicles that many Army Officers knew to be effective for their purpose, these lightweight, rugged VWs, that neither

Top *As early as 1949 the Hebmuller coachbuilding works was putting coupé bodies on the VW chassis and the demand was considerable, judging by the 49 that are seen awaiting shipment in this photograph*

Left *The rare Hebmuller drop-head coupé VW, of which only two came to the United Kingdom*

Top *Another distinct rarity—this Volkswagen coupé was constructed by Stoll of Bad Hallheim in West Germany, as a one-off exercise in 1952*

Right *An open version of the Beetle for police use, the Type 18A was produced by Hebmüller of Wüfrath in 1947/48. The roof, doors and windows were removed, the windscreen strengthened and canvas 'doors' provided for quick entry and exit*

Top *Fascia of a 1947 VW Beetle, showing the central switch for the turn-indicators, the clock matching the speedometer, and the cubby hole stowages in the metal dash*

Left *The screen pillars were somewhat obstructive but the steering-wheel was elegantly thin-rimmed*

61

Surrey Garage is British Centre for Volkswagens Parts and Service

The Volkswagen has become a not uncommon sight on British roads since the end of the war, for members of the British Army of Occupation and of the Control Commission often acquired them when on duty in Germany, and brought them back to this country.

Having taken one of these cars in part exchange for another vehicle, Managing Director A. Colborne Baber, of the Colborne Garage, Ltd., Ripley, Surrey, was so impressed with its performance that he decided to specialise in servicing and repairing Volkswagens.

After negotiations with the British concessionaire, he obtained the sole distributorship for Great Britain. At present the Board of Trade refuse to allow the importation of any new German cars, and the work of Colborne Garage therefore falls into three categories, the servicing of cars already in the country, the conversion of such cars to bring their finish more into line with British ideas, and the supplying of replacement parts.

Although there is often some delay owing to the amount of paper work required, parts are readily obtainable from the Volkswagen factory, and there is no difficulty over import licences.

Nearly forty cars have so far undergone the conversion. The vehicle is stripped right down and thoroughly inspected, then the body is re-cellulosed, the bright parts are re-chromium plated, and the seats trimmed with leather upholstery. Additional sound-proofing is also added to the engine compartment at the rear.

If required, the cars are also converted to right-hand drive, which involves raising the petrol tank in order to provide sufficient clearance for the steering box in its new position.

Price of a converted Volkswagen is £410, or £425 if modified to right-hand drive.

Reprinted from **The Garage and Motor Agent**, 6th January, 1951

Left *Colborne Baber's advertisement in* The Garage and Motor Agent *in 1951, after he had converted nearly 40 Beetles for use in Britain, started the unstemmable flood. The author had his first experience of Beetling by driving a car loaned to him by Mr A. Colborne Baber*

boiled in hot climes nor froze in winter. That is how one of the most remarkable industrial achievements of all time arose—the People's Car works of Hitler's dream soon becoming one of the finest and most prolific car-manufacturing plants in the World, at the behest of conquerors who knew that one day it would revert to German ownership! Hitler had insisted on a first-floor observation corridor $\frac{3}{4}$ mile long from which subscribers to the VW purchase plan would have been able to observe their Beetles flowing along the production lines, had the plan materialized. Years later, I was to walk that corridor, and marvel.

Top Whereas Colborne Baber charged £425 for a rhd converted VW Beetle, when the first consignments of the 'new' VW Beetles arrived in Britain, one of which is seen here, the standard model sold for £649 19s 2d and the De Luxe saloon for £739 4s 2d. W. H. T. Tayleur dealt with enquiries, from 1, Dover Street, W1. In this hand-out photograph no-one has troubled to line up the VW badge on the hub-caps!

The VW body and chassis involved expert press work and these huge Weingarten presses in the body shop at Wolfsburg were an impressive sight for anyone visiting the factory

Meanwhile, Porsche had been put in prison, falsely accused by the French of being a *criminel de guerre*, while they sought to obtain his services to assist in the creation of the Renault 4CV. His son Ferry had to design the Cisitalia racing-car for a wealthy Italian, to pay for his father's release. True burlesque stuff, providing you were not involved . . . . Meanwhile, from Wolfsburg more than 18,800 VWs emerged in 1946/47, and a trickle of exports had begun, initially to Holland and Switzerland. VW was reborn, and 1948's output of

Above *1947 VW Beetle photographed in the late 1970s. It's the Colborne-Baber car which is so well known. Obviously restored here with its sparkling chrome and two-tone paint*

Left *The Beetle, like the Morris Minor, continued with trafficators for some time even though winkers were popular. However, nothing can replace that reassuring clunk*

Above *This German registered 1952 Beetle, still with the split rear screen, has many contemporary extras*

Far *Left Very clean and perhaps over-polished there's no mistaking a very early Beetle under-hood scene. This is the 1947 Colborne-Baber car*

Left *Another 1952 Beetle in a more familiar shade of blue. Little flap cutout in front of the door can duct cool air to the driver's legs*

Right *Popular VW Owner's Club (GB) meeting known as VW Action (in this case, '81). In the foreground is a right-hand-drive 1200 Beetle. Behind it is a 1303 Cabriolet, late 1200(?), split rear window with sunroof, Beetle-based Rometsch Cabriolet and an oval rear window saloon*

Right *The most familiar 1200 engine, this one of 1960. Compact, relatively easy to maintain but usually very reliable. The Beetle featured the upright fan, other larger air-cooled VWs used the 'suitcase' flat-fan version*

*Left Volkswagenwerk
certainly hadn't killed off the
Beetle even in the mid-1970s.
This is the postcard used by
many dealers to correspond
with their customers*

Above *Some never die. 1960's
Cabriolet (untouched)
contrasts with second cousin
Porsche 911 Targa
(pampered) in Santa
Barbara, California*

Right *Mild, by American
standards, this 1300 Beetle
has received the treatment in
Britain. Perhaps the best
fitment is the wheel and tyre
combination*

Far Right *The philosophy
doesn't change. Beetles still
being made in the 1980s in
Brazil have to undergo
stringent quality control*

1981 and the real thing.
Actually made in Brazil, it's
a 1600. No VW insignia
anywhere to be seen, but then
the shape says it all

Right *Glossy Beetle brochures were ready in 1938, well before Beetles went on sale. The constant pre-launch publicity and the absurdly low forecast selling price ensured a large waiting list. Civilian deliveries, in fact, would not begin for another eight years*

Below *When it was new in the 1930s, the Beetle's platform-style chassis looked amazing futuristic. More than 60 years later, Beetles were still being built on the same basis. Petrol, front suspension, steering and spare wheel at the front, engine and transmission at the rear. Everything in between was for passengers*

VOLKSWAGEN-WERK GMBH, BERLIN

Above *This acetate overlay from the brochure rather optimistically shows five passengers and a mountain of luggage all neatly and comfortably stowed in the original Beetle saloon*

Right *During the Second World War, Porsche developed a variety of special military Beetle derivatives, including this ugly but effective machine, the Schwimmwagen (swimming-car). Not only was it a high ground-clearance liaison car, but it was designed to float in water, had a rear-mounted propeller, and could ford sizeable rivers and small lakes*

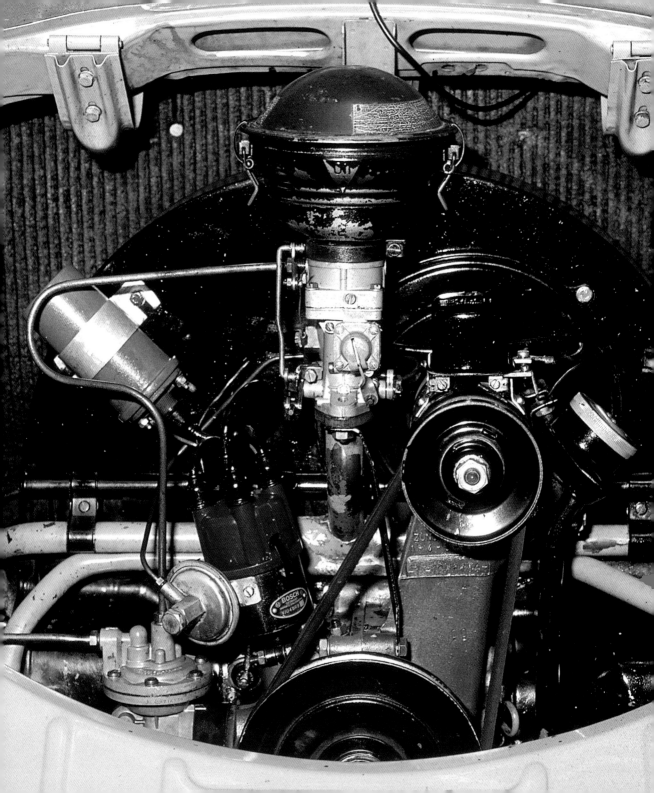

Previous page *Over the years, air-cooled Beetle engines grew from 1.0-litres to 1.6-litres, but all retained the same rear-mounted design architecture, with air-cooling in a flat-four layout. This was a 1952 example*

Above *When the New Beetle was shown at the Birmingham (NEC) Motor Show of 1998, series production of this new front-wheel-drive type had already begun. Nothing except character, and a general outline, was shared with the original Beetle, but no-one could doubt the new car's heritage*

Opposite, below *As with most cars today, the New Beetle's transversely-positioned engines were hidden under cosmetic panelling. This, in fact, was the 115bhp/2.0-litre petrol-powered 'four' – and all you can see here is the inlet manifolding, and the oil dipstick*

Above *Fast forward 60 years from the original style, and that of the new-generation Beetle looks very similar – all curves, and with the familiar sloping-back shape. In 1998, however, it was all very different under the skin, especially as a choice of engines was mounted up front, transversely-positioned, and driving the front wheels*

Above *Because the engine was mounted up front, there was of course more space in the tail, which allowed VW's designers to include a lift-up hatchback*

Right *The badge is the same, but that's about it. From behind, there was no clue that this car was based on the platform of the latest Golf hatchback and, as ever, there were suggestions of muscular wheelarches well outside the line of the cabin*

Far Right *Maybe the New Beetle shared no common components with the original, but there was no doubting its ancestry. A Bug Eye is a Bug Eye, is a Bug Eye ...*

Enthusiasts had spent years making Beetles look different, so as soon as the New Beetle was on the market VW themselves started all over again. This 1999 concept, the New Beetle RSi, featured a massive rear spoiler, different front and rear body panels, more flamboyant sill and wheelarch profiles, and spectacular alloy wheels

19,220 VWs, with 4500 exports, was to multiply quickly into millions. The British Occupation authorities kept control to September 1949, after which the plant was handed over to the Federal German Government, to be run by a Trusteeship in which the employees were represented. One of the World's greatest war-reparation prizes had escaped the British . . . .

The first VW Beetles had been shown to the Press in Berlin in February 1939; five British motoring journalists, Gordon Wilkins and Laurence Pomeroy of *The Motor*, Douglas Clease and

VWs in various stages of production-line assembly at Wolfsburg—spot welding was much in use as the bodyshells travelled along the conveyor-lines

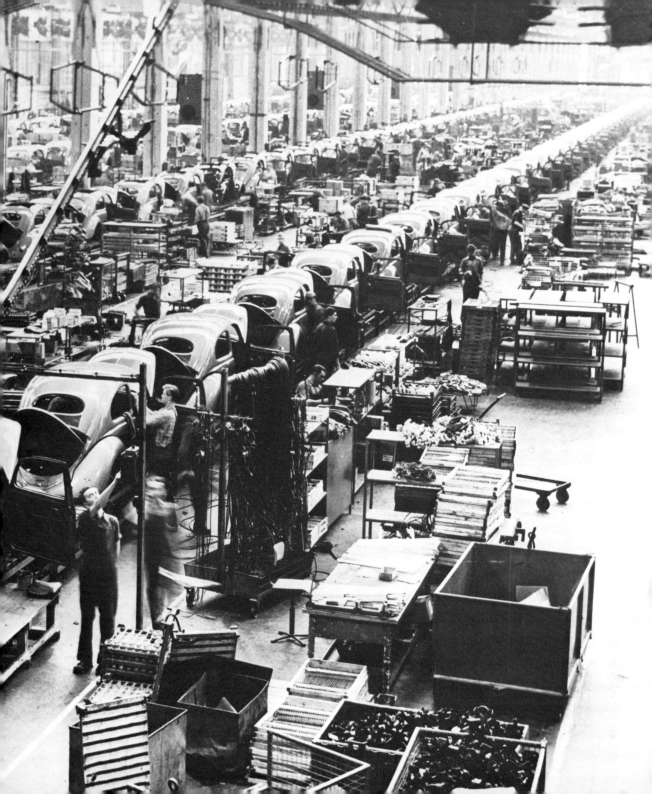

Brian Twist of *The Autocar*, and Eric Findon of *The Light Car* were present. When the project rose phoenix-like from the terrible holocaust that had been Wolfsburg, it owed its rapid success to Dr. Ing. Heinz Nordhoff, who was appointed Manager of VW by the REME Officers just before they handed over to the German Government. The re-emergence of the VW plant had owed a great deal to McEvoy, Major Ivan Hirst and Col. C. R. Radclyffe, helped materially by the one-eyed Commander Richard H. Berryman, OBE. It was a nice gesture of Lord Brabazon of Tara, when chairman of VW Motors Ltd. in Britain, to present to Mrs

Left This impressive photograph shows how multiple assembly-lines operated in the enormous Volkswagen plant at Wolfsburg, the bodyshells dropping down for attachment to the chassis

Top Dispatch of Beetles to the millions of customers— the VW factory was sited close to the canal and railway and some of the completed cars were dispatched to the agents in two-tier railway trucks

67

Above *Contrast,—away from the noise and bustle of production that was inevitable under even the ordered methods at Wolfsburg, this Beetle is seen in the peaceful setting of a country town . . .*

Below *. . . and here is an oval-rear-window Beetle being road-tested by the author for* Motor Sport, *photographed beside the sign*

for a hill up which public-road speed trials took place prior to 1925. Like the Beetle, some of the racing cars competing then were air-cooled

Far right *In the hey-day of Beetle the American importation company became well-known for some very entertaining advertising campaigns and never minded poking fun at the product if this enhanced its appeal. Here is one of their series of advertisements, proclaiming that once a Beetle owner, always a Beetle owner . . .*

Mr. Kennedy and his 1947, 1955, 1956, 1958, 1961, 1962, 1963, 1965 Volkswagen.

As long as Michael Kennedy can remember, there's always been a bug around the house.

In all, his family has owned about 15 VWs (give or take a few aunts and uncles).

So when Mr. Kennedy decided to buy one for himself, he knew enough about it to have a little fun.

He bought the body of a '47 VW and the chassis of a '55 VW. And put them together.

Then he added a '55 engine, '55 doors, '56 seats, '58 bumpers, '61 tail lights, a '62 fender, a '63 front end and a '65 transmission. (Plus a few more odds and ends.)

The 18 years' difference between the oldest part and the newest part didn't make any difference.

Many VW parts are interchangeable from one year to the next. (So there'll never be any part we can't replace in a hurry.)

If you'd rather not buy a VW the do-it-yourself way, don't worry.

At no extra charge, we'll do it ourselves.

The very memorable occasion in 1955 when the millionth VW Beetle came off the assembly lines at Wolfsburg. Somewhere in the throng of workers waiting for Herr Nordhoff to greet the millionth VW was the author, equipped with the key of the black Beetle he had left behind in England and feeling just a little claustrophobic . . .

Radclyffe the 50,000th Beetle to be imported. That was when the company had become part of the Thomas Tilling Group in 1957. It was Nordhoff, an ex-Opel man with American experience, who carried on after the British officers had prepared the way. To continue the theatrical connotation, it is said that Nordhoff arrived to apply for the job *on a bicycle.* A non-Nazi, he became Managing Director of VW, and his insistence on a one-model policy (broadened by the commercial-vehicle range), a very high quality of paintwork and an impeccable spares service, combined to ensure the success of Volkswagen throughout the World.

Top and left *The remarkable display outside the factory on 6 August 1955 to commemorate the production of one-million Volkswagens since the end of the war. Were they real cars, or models?*

Chapter 6
Nostalgia

I first became aware of the funny little motorised Beetle when Army personnel who had used military versions in the field, or who had seen the first production saloons, wrote to *Motor Sport* about it. At this time the specification of the Beetle was regarded as highly unconventional, and therefore to be regarded with suspicion by British car users. Air-cooling had been known but had virtually died with the cyclecar, but did appear to thrive in the fan-induced Franklin of America with their $4\frac{1}{2}$-litre air-cooled sixes, and even a V12 in the early 1930s. Rear-engined cars were being reintroduced by Renault and others, for very small cars, but the engine-in-the-boot had otherwise been confined mainly to oddballs like our queer Burney Streamline and Crossley saloons, or the big Tatra from Czechoslovakia. Thus, the front-engined, water-cooled car ruled the roost.

Only those less staid in their technical thinking accepted the VW. Among them was A. J. Colborne Baber, a vintage Bentley driver, who distributed imported VWs to the US Forces at Manston Air Base in the early 1950s. When I asked for a car to test I was told that so continuous was the demand for Beetles that he couldn't spare one, even for a few hours. However, when he flew to Wolfsburg on business, he allowed me to sample his own 1947 Beetle, finished in two shades of blue which his son Peter

still owns. After 350 miles, including a trip to the Goodwood (car) races, I was captivated. The odd little car went up to an indicated 70 mph and gave 36 mpg. For his military VWs Dr. Porsche had increased the engine size to 1131 cc, from March 1943, which capacity the post-war Beetle had inherited. At the time you couldn't purchase VWs for sterling, but Mr. Baber overhauled used ones

The picture on page 8 shows the frontage of the London VW showrooms in St. John's Wood. This is the main service station behind the showrooms in Lodge Road, not far from Lord's cricket ground, where the author used to go for VW servicing

73

The quick-service facilities and Castrol lubrication-bay at the Lord's Court, London, VW service depot

at his Colborne Garage at Ripley in Surrey, selling them at prices ranging from £425 to £475, his Works Manager W. R. Howden having taken the Mechanics' Course in Germany. I began to learn all the delights of the Beetle—the car's body so well sealed that you had to open a window slightly before the doors would shut easily, how clean the boxer-engine kept in its air-tight rear compartment, the easy gear shift, the light steering, the up-to-40 mpg petrol economy, and the splendidly glossy paint finish. (Likely to be painted in England—other 'standard' Beetles had matte appearances.) Forward visibility was good over the curved bonnet, rear vision less so through a small back window, divided on early cars. I was prepared to overlook the restricted luggage capacity, confined to the under-bonnet space shared with the spare wheel, and a deep but narrow well behind the back seat. There was the bonus of a really large (8.8 gallon) front-mounted fuel tank with an enormous filler orifice, through which you felt you could pass a hand to remove obstructions! Moreover, there was a reserve fuel-tap. And the double trailing-arm, torsion-bar front-independent suspension was so like that of the Auto Union Grand Prix cars that the VW's rear engine location seemed entirely logical. . . .

This Colborne-Baber Beetle had a non-synchromesh gearbox and cable-operated brakes. I decided that when hydraulic brakes and synchromesh became available, the Beetle was for me. This desire was enhanced when VWs became officially represented here, promoted by Stephen O'Flaherty in 1953, from a small office in London. This British franchise led to the formation of VW Motors Ltd. with new showrooms at Byron House, 7/9 St. James's Street, in London's fashionable West End. In 1953 the new company provided me with a road-test Beetle, from which I obtained speeds of 23, 41, 56, and 71 mph in the forward gears, and 36 mpg, cruising at 65 mph. The price with purchase-tax was then £739 4s 2d. I like the 2d (12 old pence=five New P). Prior to this, O'Flaherty had run an import business in VWs in Dublin, later assembling them there.

Volkswagen were already building up a fine reputation for a sound spares-service, and quite early on over 200 UK distributors and dealers had been signed-on. I remember a friend who had run a

Top A few more years, and five million VWs had emerged from Wolfsburg and been scattered about the world

Right The large tyres and rear-engine location give the Beetle a good grip on snow. Here one sees a very standard-looking model competing in the 1961 Monte Carlo Rally, under snowy conditions

substantial Jowett agency telling me he had changed to VW when the Bradford make faded out and that before he so much as saw a VW he was made to purchase a comprehensive supply of VW spares. This seemed unnecessary at the time, but was the only way to get the agency. Then, one day, a farmer called in, who owned an old VW Commercial, saying it was imperative to get to market but something vital had broken. And, lo, there in the spares store was the part he required, in stock, and he departed a confirmed VW user.... That was a measure of the strength behind the Volkswagen sales-drive.

Sales were going well from St. James's Street, under Mr. Dear. I tried another Beetle in 1953, the

Snow again—and a 1963 Beetle equipped for autobahn patrol

price now down to £698. For 1954 many subtle improvements were made. The engine-size was increased to 1192 cc, by increasing the cylinder bore to 77 mm from 75 mm, the piston stroke remaining at 64 mm. This raised the power from 25 bhp at 3300 rpm to 30 bhp at 3400 rpm, as the compression-ratio had been increased from 5.8 to 6.1:1, the inlet passages cleared up, valve diameter enlarged from 28 mm to 30 mm, and many

The larger rear window, bigger rear lamps and twin plated exhaust tail-pipes of the VW 1200 of 1965 are seen to good effect here, also the effective back bumper

minor changes carried out. The low-revving VW engine was expected to go 70,000 miles without requiring a re-bore. Dynamo output, for the admittedly 6-volt electrical system was up from 130 to 160 watts, the Solex 28PICT carburettor had been adjusted to suit the greater engine size, and

A year later the 1500 model was virtually indistinguishable from the smaller-engined Beetle, except for the badge on the bonnet-lid

Formula-Vee racing was made possible at notably low cost by using the VW engine in a racing single seater such as this. VW Motors now operated from Volkswagen House in South Norwood, on the outskirts of S.E. London and H.E. Whitaker looked after racing enquiries, for a class of the sport that was thriving in America, Sweden and Germany, as well as in Britain

an oil-bath air-cleaner added, the inlet manifold was better served with hot-spotting, and the Bosch ignition distributor provided with vacuum as well as centrifugal advance-and-retard control.

The engine was, however, still stifled deliberately in its breathing ability, as on a Model-T Ford, in the interests of preventing over-revving, and as every VW engine was run for some 20 minutes on the bench at Wolfsburg, no running-in was called for. Mr. Dear entered a Beetle (No. 119) in the 1954 RAC Rally, in which it finished the course, doing approximately 35 mpg on Shell 74-octane fuel and using only $\frac{3}{4}$ of a pint of Shell X100 oil, although the engine had seen but 434 miles at the start of the Rally, 2469 miles at the finish, after which I was allowed to drive the car for another 378 miles, to prove that this particular Beetle was now becoming a little looser, and that the lower top-gear ratio (3.61 against the former 3.5:1) made for better pick-up.

During this test the Sekurit windscreen disintegrated for some unknown reason, although it was possible to see through the glass before it collapsed. This reminds me that on another VW the same thing happened, but due to an overloaded truck dropping a stone on the bonnet, which I saw bounce off and hit the screen. I wrote to the truck's operators, asking for compensation. They agreed, providing I quoted the Reg. No. of the offending vehicle. I had been unable to see it as the glass shattered but a visit to the contractor's yard enabled me to quote a registration number at random from a row of lorries parked there on a Sunday afternoon, and all was well! Good comes out of evil, too, they say; I was on my way to the Road Research Laboratory when the screen

Right *Mr S. H. Grylls, ex-Chief Engineer of Rolls-Royce Motors and directly respoinsible for the Rolls-Royce Silver Shadow, bought a VW Beetle He used it with undisguised enthusiasm for many years*

shattered, and their scientists were delighted, begging samples of the particles that remained in the car, as apparently it would enable them to learn something vital about German toughened glass!

The more I studied VW Beetles, the more convinced I became that I wanted one. The ingenious air-cooled engine had a very clever oil-cooling system, apart from which it was always fun to open the rear lid and find very little therein that resembled a conventional power-unit. Even the handbook was delightfully produced.

Another thing that endeared the Volkswagen organization to me was its very thorough Customer-relations Service. Mr James Graydon,

These 1302S Beetles were provided for Finnish motoring journalists to test at the time of the debut of this new model in 1970. Note the studded tyres

Left By 1970 Formula-Vee racing cars were using Beetle engines tuned to give 95 bhp and some 3000 had been built, only five years after Gerhard Mitter, European Mountain Champion had first driven a 1200 cc FV car in Europe

looking like an avuncular bank manager, was now in charge in London, operating with a quiet efficiency that was as efficient as it was unpretentious. I believe he came from Rootes, who could so easily have had VW for themselves. By now there was a big spares store located at first at 78/85 Davies Street, W1 then in London's East End dockland, at Plaistow E15, in the charge of another pleasant fellow, where a new paint shop was added in 1957. The Headquarters in Wolfsburg never failed to reply in great detail to the most outrageous technical enquiries, apart from which they awarded medals and commemorative wrist watches to those owners of Beetles whose original engines and transmissions ran for 100,000 kilometres without major repair— the medals were for attaching to the VW steel facia. But the item that set the seal on this Teutonic thoroughness was when they slightly altered the shape of the Beetle's petrol tank and made its filler a bit smaller. No other changes at that moment, so no call to alter the instruction-book. Yet when you unfurled its colour plate of the Beetle in sideview, it was to find that the fuel tank and filler had been correctly redrawn. Marvellous! As was the presentation of a brand-new Beetle to the owner of the oldest, best-kept example to be found, when this was wanted for the Lord Montagu's Motor Museum at Beaulieu; I remember judging this, in the presence of his Lordship and Mr. Graydon.

So in 1955 I became a Beetle-man. I chose a black-Beetle, because I regarded the VW as the universal Model-T Ford's legitimate successor, and that immortal auto was originally offered, you remember, in 'any colour so long as it's black'. I proudly took delivery from St. James's Street but by the time I had got to Staines bridge, heading for Hampshire, I began to have doubts about the

Sea-going. The Beetle had a notably waterproof and draught proof body (you needed to open the window to shut the doors easily) and this prompted some courageous sea-crossing frolics. This Beetle, captained by Malc Buchanan, set off across the Irish Sea from the Isle of Man heading for England, aided by the addition of a water-propeller. It ran out of fuel 4 miles off-shore but was blown to its destination by a favourable wind. If you have to drop into a river, choose a Beetle in which to go aquatic!

CHAPTER SIX

An aerial view of the truly impressive VW factory, one of Hitler's dreams, and in which there was a viewing gallery from which favoured visitors could watch assembly taking place on the mile-long assembly-lines

Top Later Beetle refinements—more interior space, the petrol-filler cap concealed under a flap, and greater areas of glass, rubber-ribbed bumpers and outsized rear lamps

Right In the more intense rallies in Europe the irrepressible VW Beetle was often to the fore—this one was rallied by Team Austria in 1972

handling provided by the swing-axle, independent-rear-suspension. The problem proved simple. I had been despatched with far too little air in the Michelins . . . . The only non-standard items I had on this 1192 cc de luxe Beetle were a spot-lamp and a neat and steady-reading fuel gauge, additional precaution to kicking over to reserve with the floor-mounted petrol tap, which released another 1.1 gallons.

The large tyres on the Beetle ensured the same lack of wear on the rubber as the low crankshaft-speed delayed deterioration of the engine. There were problems, though. During the 16,000 miles I covered during the first year I had the insect (there were many other cars to drive as

well) the wipers failed coming back from Snetterton (the wiper motor was not by Bosch on my car). Later, the oil cooler split, dousing the engine with Castrol. I stopped outside the immaculate Mayfair VW showrooms with the boot-lid up. A salesman rushed out quickly and shut it, before anti-Volkswagen folk could add more ammunition to their arguments. But being VW, they openly admitted that the early coolers suffered from faulty welding and promised to fit a later version the same day. When a front-wheel bearing packed up, again, no excuses, just a quick service. In the end, many hundreds of miles later, another well-known malady struck – a timing gear stripped and a tow home was necessary.

Yet another failure occurred when a key stripped in one of the timing-gears, at a time when my Beetle was overdue for servicing. That was a pity, as I had persuaded a nice young girl to come out with me, the inducement being a flight in a friend's DH Tiger Moth from Fairoaks Aerodrome. We never got there! Seeing my plight, and wrath, an MG owner came out of his workshop, heard my story, and generously made me up a replacement key on the spot. That stoppage was at 16,067 miles, and was actually caused by my carelessness when trying to replace a broken fan-belt; the next belt lasted much longer. As the new key was unhardened I decided it ought to be replaced with a VW key and went to a dealer in Staines to get one. The demand for this tiny, inexpensive spare caught them out—they could have supplied body panels and wings and crankcases and such things, under the conscientious VW spares scheme—but not this humble little key!

Beetling, after you had caught the bug, was the greatest fun. Fellow owners would flash their headlamps at you as you converged, and even stop

Top and left *The lines they loved. Note the hooded headlamps, wing-top side-lamps and ventilated disc wheels of this 1973 1303 Beetle. The big rear lamps and rear number-plate illumination show up well in this picture*

to help if trouble struck. In this context, I was motoring disconsolately through London one evening after my wife had gone to a dance, (a pastime not to my taste), when I saw a considerable length of attractive female leg protruding from another Beetle. I stopped, naturally. It transpired that the lady was stranded with a broken clutch cable, not immediately repairable. But she accepted a lift and I had bacon-and-eggs in her Kensington flat, that day and subsequently. (In view of the foregoing anecdotes, perhaps I should say that I am still happily married!)

Looking back, the 1192 cc Beetle was slow, and care was needed when cornering quickly (that swing-axle over-steer) but Michelin 'X' on the back wheels helped. The driving stance was

cramped, luggage difficult to load, the heater smelly. The battery was located under the back seat, presumably to reduce voltage drop to the starter. We were careless in leaving its cover off and this caused our Saint Bernard, a heavy animal, to start a fire when the frame of the seat shorted the terminals; the rapid exit of wife and self, no less by the dog, remains in my memory. Yet after it had been retired by me my VW continued into an astronomical-mileage in other hands and when my three daughters became motorists I went to the aforesaid ex-Jowett dealer and bought a very clean one-lady-owner Beetle for them, the hydraulic-braked model. They put on a roof rack, overloaded it unmercifully, and thrashed it across Europe laden with boy friends

1974 saw the return of the 'basic' Beetle but, as is obvious, it was not so basic as the early postwar cars

as part of the holiday adjuncts. The only fault was a 'flat' battery, because they omitted to top it up. When the engine finally showed signs of expiring, an inexpensive rebuild was undertaken very satisfactorily by Autocarvan, then a very small concern on the outskirts of Aldershot, but now a prosperous VW spares business.

Even with hindsight I can say the VW was a very good car indeed in its day. The tyre paint was still wet on the Michelins when I took delivery of mine, and two days later I was at a VW Owners Club *Concours d'Elegance*, which can be construed as showing off! In later times the VW Service Station moved to St. John's Wood, close to Lords Cricket Ground in London, and it was always a pleasure to collect one's newly-serviced Beetle from there; they had a waiting room for the customers, just as if we were lordly Rover 'uncles and aunts' using Rover's Seagrave Road depot. There was one funny episode, when the unsuspecting Mobil Oil people tried to interest me in taking the Beetle to their London depot for a free flush-out and refill with the new Permazone antifreeze(!). And there was a happy visit with my wife to Wolfsburg in August 1955 to see the 1,000,000th VW Beetle come off the factory assembly-line. I wrote of this at the time and I have no reason to alter anything that I said then:

In the early afternoon of August 5th the millionth VW came off the assembly lines of the Volkswagenwerk at Wolfsburg. This significant milestone in production of the post-war VW was made the occasion of a festival weekend concluding the annual works' holiday, to which an enormous concourse of international motoring correspondents, journalists and VW distributors and dealers, 1,000 in all, were invited, and which embraced celebrations in a specially-constructed stadium at which 160,000 persons were said to be present.

For us this memorable occasion commenced with a very early start from Heathrow on the Friday in a K.L.M. Convair 240, which flew forty journalists and trade representatives from England, Scotland, and Ireland comfortably, at 9,000 feet and 238 m.p.h., to Hanover Airport.

On arrival at Hanover Teutonic efficiency stepped in, in earnest. To meet the foreign visitors were an impressive line of thirty VW Microbuses, backed by huge Mercedes-Benz and Skoda coaches, each having a guide who was allocated to his party for the entire weekend, while all luggage, coats and the inevitable odds and ends could be left in the 'bus at all times, each Microbus carrying a number for identification, and being under guard the whole time.

This convoy set out impressively along the Dusseldorf-Berlin autobahn, past Lehrte, Peine and Braunschweig, where the Bussing lorry factory is situated, to Wolfsburg, at a cruising speed of some 60 m.p.h., these remarkable 1.2-litre air-cooled buses, each with eight or nine occupants, keeping close station, aided by efficient brakes, until we turned off for the factory, with a five-sail windmill and the new hospital

The VW engine that powered the Beetle had many uses, such as in light aeroplanes, and the Beetle itself appeared in many non-beetle-like guises, including the beach-buggies, the elegant Karmann Ghia coupés and, of course, the Transporter versions. Here is a more unexpected use for the tough flat-four air-cooled VW engine—powering one of the sand rails in the exciting Baja 1000 race on California's Mexican peninsula

on the hill overlooking the woods as landmarks, into Wolfsburg, a town en fete, its green and white flags greeting us on all sides. Here we were ushered into the factory's vast new assembly hall, and after about half an hour saw the eine million Volkswagen come off the line, after speeches by a representative of the workers and by Dr. Ing. h.c. Heinz Nordhoff himself, who performed the simple ceremony of fixing the appropriate chassis-number plaque to the car, a gold-plated saloon which glistened in the concentrated light of the arc-lamps for the Press and cinema cameras.

That Nordhoff is popular with the workers there was no doubt, as cheer after cheer greeted his arrival and his address, and happy laughter his efforts in riveting the aforesaid number-plate. We were beginning also to perceive the efficiency which pervades Wolfsburg and has enabled this vast production of motorcars to take place in a factory that was 60 per cent a war-bombed shambles only ten years ago. Here we were, standing beside this assembly-line on this momentous occasion, our journey from Britain, including miles of autobahn, perfectly timed, a neat VW eine million badge in our buttonhole, a map of our journey and a little pro-gramme in English in our hand, each one signed by Nordhoff, and the whole undertaking staged with a minimum of fuss—and a complete absence of policing. Indeed, throughout the weekend the only officials we noticed about the works were calm, smiling works-police.

After this we were conducted to a huge and very pleasant dining hall, used normally as a staff canteen, for lunch. We were fortunate in sitting with Major and Mrs. Hirst, for Major Hirst had been at Wolfsburg with the British Forces after the war and was able to give us interesting details of how the unique VW organization came into being.

That afternoon was devoted to a conducted tour of the factory. It would take a week to see fully over this vast— and I can justifiably write fantastic—plant, and it would merit an article at least three times the length of this one to do it justice. In the two hours at our disposal

it was impossible to inspect everything, and we missed seeing the body-priming and engine-assembly, although nothing seemed to be out of bounds save the experimental department. From the astounding overhead observation corridor (ordered by Hitler so that his people would see the cars he was building for them!), with its floor of black and white check and doors of wrought iron and glass, which runs for three-quarters of a mile along the factory wall, there is a view of this great plant, which instead of being split up as is the practice in Britain, occupies vast halls, very clean, very spacious and lofty, lit by daylight. Here, in normal times — for this was a holiday week — nearly 30,000 workers (of whom eight per cent were salaried staff) accommodated in 5,300 new flats in the growing town of Wolfsburg, which has a 40,000 population, are turning out one vehicle every minute of the working day, for six days a week, to achieve an output which has risen from 713 cars to one million cars in the space of ten years, the greatest automobile output achieved in Europe since the war.

As far as the eye could see were the great Weingarten body presses, finished body-shells being pushed on tubular trolleys to the overhead gantrys which carry them to the chassis assembly lines. Welding of every description goes on in covered bays, the fuel tank being welded-up automatically. Raw materials arrive in railway trucks at siding within the factory, and in great barges up the canal which runs alongside. And swarf and metal waste is swept away through holes in the floor, keeping the factory as clean as a racing-car shop. Small parts, finished on batteries of Scharer lathes, are conveyed, at fearful speed by extremely skilled hands driving highly-manoeuvrable Clark trucks, to the assembly points. The finished cars come off four parallel roller-assembly-lines, headlamps being adjusted before a marked screen, which swings aside to let the VW roll down a short ramp which starts the engine. It is driven a few yards to a testing machine, the front wheels being aimed against chocks, a hook rising automatically out of the floor to attach itself to the back of the car, so that the driver can check horsepower output at the back

wheels, which revolve on rollers sunk into the floor. This test occupies only a few minutes, the engine having been run-in on the bench, before the car is driven off to the great outdoor storage parks—for the VW is intended to withstand the elements and doesn't require a garage. I understand that a tolerance of 5 h.p. is permitted at this final check, most cars showing about 30 b.h.p. at the back wheels. Darting in and around the assembly bays were occasional chassis, with circular fuel tanks clipped on, their drivers handling them at speed as any motoring enthusiast would love to have done, their purpose being to make spot checks on the general run of chassis flowing along the production lines. In the vast halls that comprise the VW factory no undue noise and no fumes were evident from the indoor testing of chassis and finished cars.

Rivalling the Model-T Ford as a universal car, the Beetle has been put to many uses. This one has replaced the agricultural tractor or horse for pulling the plough on a Mexican farm, equipped with 'slicks' to increase its already celebrated slippery-surface traction

*An aerial view of a VW
export shipping facility, at
the height of the Beetle boom.
VW even owned its own
ships to transport fleets of
cars to North America*

The Volkswagen Beetle as so many of us remember it, and which is still encountered so frequently on the roads and in the cities all over the Globe—this 1200 cc model which was also available with the 1.6-litre engine. One of the last made in Germany

Some way from the main factory is another great hall housing the power plant, steam from which is used not only to heat the factory but also the town of Wolfsburg.

Those are just superficial impressions of a walk through the Wolfsburg factory, where 1,280 vehicles, including 190 to 200 Microbuses and transporters, are made every day.

After this tour, with which no one, whether pro- or anti-VW, could fail to be deeply impressed, we were taken in our 'buses to the other end of the factory for Dr.

*Nordhoff's Press conference. This took place in a huge
and tastefully laid-out lecture hall with built-in mic-
rophone installations for use by the assembled journalists at question-time, and it was here that what was
probably the largest congregation of international
Pressmen ever assembled at a motor-car factory heard
Dr. Nordhoff deliver his address, a copy of which, in
perfect English (it occupied 20 typewritten quarto
pages), had been handed to us as we entered.*

    Having spent my schooldays idly day-dreaming of

Brooklands and Le Mans, I was not, alas, equipped to follow all the questions which followed this speech, but I was told by the Foreign Correspondent of one of the great London newspapers that Nordhoff parried very skilfully the awkward ones appertaining to who owns VW and when will a balance-sheet be published? Nor have I space to publish his address in full, but he said some extremely sound and commonsense things. For example, he acknowledged that VW realizes it cannot produce one car more than their Sales Organization is able to sell somewhere in the world and consequently not a single car leaves the works without a buyer having paid for it in full. In 1948 they had 40 distributors in Germany and one abroad. Today, the figures are 1,000 in Germany and 2,800 abroad, and, without being presumptuous, Nordhoff said he could claim the best Sales and Service Organization in Europe, and no feeling of inferiority when comparing it with similar organizations in the U.S.A.

This year VW would export an average of 55 per cent of its production, or approximately 35,000 VWs to U.S.A., 28,000 to Sweden, 18,000 to Belgium, 14,000 to Holland, 12,000 to Switzerland and 10,000 to Austria. "Yet," said Nordhoff, "we are far from sitting on top of the world". He went on to outline worries of coal and steel shortages and the workers' desire for a five-day week, which he does not think possible for another four or five years. He spent much time on a vicious attack on Germany's road-repairing policy, calling for better roads, as we do here, and saying he doesn't believe that there is insufficient money available. He made the unique offer to subscribe "a not inconsiderable sum towards road loans" if a co-ordinated and long-term plan could be agreed upon. In attacking speed-limits and road faults, Nordhoff called for a ten-year programme of road improvement and said what he spoke of he observed not "as one who sits in the back seat of a luxurious chauffer-driven limousine, but as one who has observed personally and experienced these things in driving a VW 25,000 to 40,000 miles every year." Germany, he said, with the exception of approximately

1,400 miles of autobahn, has 160,000 miles of town and country roads which originate, at best, from the late Middle Ages. Traffic would increase—already VW workers own about 2,000 VWs—and more cars could be sold if the roads were built and repaired to accommodate them—words that came forcibly home to us as we grappled with Sunday-morning congestion through Staines and along A30 after our return home!

Tribute was paid to the late Professor Porsche, who designed the VW and who once said to Nordhoff, towards the end of his too-short life, "Only since you proved it do I know that I was right," and to the late Dr. Feuereissen who, in building up the VW organization had, Nordhoff said, "created a monument to himself which will last longer than bronze or stone, a monument of accomplishment and success, and a reminder of his deep human kindness and sincerity." (Major Hirst had told us at lunch of how he had introduced Uhlenhaut to Feuereissen when the former had paid a visit to Wolfsburg, and how he had seen the former rival racing car engineers of Mercedes-Benz and Auto Union depart arm-in-arm in enthralled conversation!)

Nordhoff said that for 65 years there has been a European automobile industry and connected with it are names having an historical ring; but to pass the millionth production mark for the first time in Europe since the end of the war with one and the same type of car has been reserved for one of its youngest factories, the Volkswagenwerk. This has often been misleadingly called an "economic miracle," but in fact it is due only to hard work and a determination to achieve things. In answer to a question, Nordhoff said he faced the greatest competition from British cars. "Hard work and determination," concluded Nordhoff, "has always been the strong point of the Germans, for we enjoy working if we know for what purpose, and I should think that everyone who has lived through the last 15 catastrophic years really does know for what purpose."

After the address Nordhoff joined his guests for dinner in a huge hall normally used for indoor car testing, visitors being grouped in nations at long tables decorated with the appropriate flag, and the hall dominated by huge flags hanging from inclined masts, colourful in the quiet neon-lighting, as armies of waiters served food and wine. Late that night the convoy of thirty VW Microbuses set out along the autobahn for Hanover, this impressive sight enhanced now that tail-lamps glowed for a mile on end and warm light flooded the roadside from the windows of the speeding vehicles. Nordhoff had said harsh things in his speech about police traps and the absence of traffic police after 6 p.m., but certainly we had a very capable police escort of white-coated rider on a B.M.W. motor-cycle—the motor-cycle police of most nationalities display extreme skill in convoy-accompanying of this sort.

What remained of the Friday night was spent in a delightful room at the Hotel Waterloo, with adjacent black-tiled bathroom. In the morning (after a short shopping expedition, during which my wife bought an excellent German folding umbrella for £1 and I restricted myself economically to the purchase of a Mercedes-Benz 170 Siku toy), our fleet of 'buses took us back to Wolfsburg via the nearly-completed VW factory just outside Hanover.

Here is emphasis of VW efficiency and drive. At present Microbuses and transporters are made at one end of the Wolfsburg factory, but by the end of October this new factory will take over VW commercial vehicle production, commencing with 3,000 existing Wolfsburg employees and absorbing local labour. It took us quite a long time to circle the new buildings, which are set in open country not unduly spoiled by them, with blocks of workers' flats adjacent, yet the building time is scheduled as a mere 27 weeks, and by the middle of 1956 it is planned to build there 300 VW transporters a day. The cost of the new factory will be £10-million. Incidentally, there is a great demand for these useful air-cooled vehicles throughout Germany, and we were told that the thirty brand-new ones used to transport us during our visit would sell easily at slightly less than list price after our departure.

We again journeyed, police-escorted, along the auto-

bahn to Wolfsburg, the primitive farming in the wide, flat fields contrasting sharply with the efficiency which lay ahead! Mercedes-Benz, D.K.W. Sonderklasse, Opel and occasional B.M.W. sang along the German motor-roads, and, of course, those vast transporters mit trailers, many of which wore proudly the Mercedes-Benz star on their radiator caps. In Hanover, as elsewhere, VWs predominate, but I saw a couple of Austins and one early M.G. Vintage cars are not understood there and my "score" was confined to some rather ancient Goliath three-wheeler vans and other commercials, although quite a number of pre-war two-cylinder D.K.W.s and B.M.W.s are still about. The

The air-cooled Beetle in its 1980s form. Although German assembly ended in 1978, millions of cars were later built in Brazil and Mexico. This one was made in Mexico, for sale in Germany

trams use overhead wires and often pull twin trailers!

After lunch in the same vast hall (at the end of which each guest was presented with a scale model of a VW car or commercial, specially made by Wiking-Modellbau of Berlin, the body of which detached to show the location of engine, seats, petrol tank and spare wheel), we walked to the stadium on this sunny Saturday afternoon for the festival performance—walked down the long grass-flanked avenues outside the factory, where Nordhoff's special roses bloom in the flower-beds, past enormous beer-gardens where that evening the VW workers and their families and friends would receive free beer to the accompaniment of music by the Irish Guards—the tables, chairs and glasses had been prepared the day before and everything stood serenely in place, not a table overturned, not a glass broken during the night. In this well-ordered, well-behaved town, where Nordhoff lives in a flat amongst his treasured collection of jade, the townsfolk on this day were allowed to walk their wives, children and friends round the factory.

Let me explain about the stadium! It was built by VW specially for the occasion. Some 160,000 persons entered it without policing or red tape, the more honoured visitors seated on vast stands of wooden construction, that stood up safely to the enormous numbers who occupied them. Above a tastefully-decorated open-air stage hands sped over the dials of four clocks, and as each nation's representative pressed buttons the hands stopped opposite numbers, to give a figure that was promptly displayed on a board adjacent. These numbers were those of lucky ticket-holders in Wolfsburg who had won a free VW, ten in all being presented in this way. In addition, during Friday the workers had driven about the streets in flower-decked VWs wearing huge numbers, and those guessing correctly which number would appear first at given points won other VWs as prizes!

The festival performance was ably compered by the inexhaustible Novotny, on whose broad shoulders the bulk of the weekend's fantastically complicated organization—complete even to the English-worded

By the 1980s, Mexican-built Beetles were being sold in Germany, where production had ended in 1978. By 1982 a 1200L cost 8991 DM, which was about £2200, or 4500 US Dollars, a real bargain. As with all German-build VWs, build quality was very high

card in our bedroom in Hanover wishing us goodnight on behalf of VW!—had fallen.

In this flag-decked stadium—VW had ensured fine weather!—performances were given by bands and/or dancers from eleven different nations, each visiting VW main distributor making a short speech and pressing the aforementioned buttons to give away another VW to a lucky prizewinner. I am proud to state that the band of the Irish Guards, under Capt. C. H. Jaeger and its Commandant, Col. D. M. L. Gordon-Watson, O.B.E., M.C., was particularly well received, the Germans amongst the spectators beating time to the martial music. They loudly applauded the Highland dancers of Jack McConachie. Stephen O'Flaherty, Chairman of VW Motors Ltd. of London and Director of the Dublin VW distributors, spoke capably on behalf of Great Britain. Zulu dancers had been flown in from Africa at a cost of £800, M. S. Brooks, Managing Director of South African Motor Assemblers and Distributors Ltd., making a forceful speech on behalf of South Africa, some of it in Zulu! Popular indeed was the modern Camino band from South America, accompanied by scantily-clad dancing girls. So this fine spectacle unfolded. Here, in a packed stadium, the entertainers of Switzerland, Sweden, South Africa, Belgium, South America, Great Britain, France, Holland, America, Austria and Germany performed, in that sequence, in harmony before this vast international gathering, on a spot which a decade before was the scene of bombing, mutiny by refugees and endless hardship and privation.

Today the VW organization is unique. It is owned by no one, is neither a socialist nor a capitalist undertaking, inasmuch as the State and the workers do not control it, yet all its profits are ploughed back into making more and more VWs and publicising them. Out of bad has come good. Can it be that Providence has, just this once, chosen Wolfsburg for a demonstration of what can be achieved when the executives and the workers toil for a common cause, in a form of socialism which is yet no sop to the socialism of politics?

It is worth pondering on, whether you are anti-German and intend to slate me for publicizing the VW, or whether you consider, with us, that a journalist should be beyond politics and attempt to report accurately what he sees. For VW has produced 30,000 happy workers where previously discontent and poverty prevailed. In 1954 the factory's turnover amounted to eleven hundred million marks. I understand that its workers are paid wages about equal to those paid for equivalent work in Coventry. They have a fine new town, flanked by unspoilt woodland. And, as the VWs, cars and commercials, saloon and convertible, some with "winkers" and strengthened bumpers for the American market, pour into the storage parks and away to the world's buyers, all Germany benefits from an organization the like of which has never been seen before and perhaps never will be elsewhere. Out of the horrors of destruction of war has come a well-knit, contented, proud community, working for a common cause under the command of the remarkable and well-loved Heinz Nordhoff. It could be that Providence has lifted the curtain, pointing the way . . . I do not know. I am only a motoring journalist. But I wonder!

The VW programme embraces a slight reduction in exports so as to provide more VWs for the German market, at reduced price, so that a German can buy a standard-model VW for about £315. No change in the cars is anticipated for a least the next million vehicles! Consequently, low depreciation is assured. Nor will the factory at Wolfsburg, which in recent times has been extended by the erection of new buildings covering some 320,000 square yards, be allowed to grow much larger. Already there exist firm sales contracts for six months ahead, and demand exceeds supply.

The aim will be to continue to supply the world with a reliable, economical family car, impervious to heat or cold, able to live in the open without harm, and capable of running 60,000 miles without major repairs. (Nordhoff remarked that 120,000 miles isn't looked upon with astonishment.) In spite of an absence of transfer drilling machines and the like, VW engines and cars will be turned out in increasing numbers—and the increase has been in the order of 40,036 in 1945–48, 86,190 by 1949, 176,228 by 1950, 281,940 by 1951, 417,953 by 1952, 597,693 by 1953, 840,066 by 1954, to 1,000,000 early in August, 1955. Nordhoff said: "The American public likes our cars, and we must therefore take the necessary steps before making our preliminary plans for 1956 to ensure that she will get them." But he hopes to stabilize exports at 50 per cent. of production, "a proportion that should be fair to all concerned".

I consider that the air-cooled, all-independently-

sprung, rear-engined VW is the finest all-round small family car, everything considered, so I was pleased to learn that when the factory re-opened on August 7th to build cars from 1,000,001 onwards, there would be minor improvements in respect of just those features which have in the past been open to criticism. These take the form of a slightly thinner seat back giving more legroom in the back compartment, a change of interior trim giving about the same increase in width, different door locks to prevent rattling, and a changed shape of petrol tank so that, while it still holds that useful nine gallons with reserve supply, it gives 20 per cent greater luggage space under the bonnet. In addition, dual, plated exhaust pipes are now standard, the rear and brake lamps have been improved, brighter finish and upholstery colours are available, and the driver's seat squab angle is adjustable on the Export model to three different positions.

The saloon (called a limousine in Germany) and Karmann convertible remain the normal models, but the much-discussed Karmann-Ghia coupé was on show on the Saturday. This has very attractive lines and does 75 m.p.h. with the standard engine, a speed which will no doubt be increased by the fitting of two-carburettor conversion, etc. I understand that this coupé will sell in this country for under £1,200 and will be on show on the VW stand at Earls Court next month, where, as a sort of "poor man's Porsche," it should create a profound interest.

So ended this remarkable Eine-Million *Festival, the preparations for which had occupied Novotny and his staff for eight months. It remained only to say goodbye to our guide, Hermann Flath, normally a Middle-East VW fieldman, and let K.L.M. fly us home, via Amsterdam, for a night's sleep. At London Airport I bade farewell to Mr. J. Graydon, Manager of VW Motors Ltd. in London, who had worked so hard to ensure the success of our visit, and drove home in My VW Beetle, which, in 8,000 hard-driven miles, has cost 3s. 8d. for repairs—for a new stop-light bulb.*

I have no reason to be frantically pro-German but I

should be sub-human if this journey to Wolfsburg had left me unimpressed.

Incidentally, I believe that when it was realized that there was no example of the then brand-new Karmann Ghia VW coupé at Wolfsburg one was rushed from the Karmann body-building plant at Osnabrück through the night a distance of some 180 miles, typical of the VW efficiency under Nordhoff. . . . And I confess I felt some apprehension for the future of my children on this occasion of German thoroughness and efficiency—as the present proves not to have been without foundation.

A Mexican-built 1200L VW Beetle lines up alongside some of the later products of the VW-Audi organization at Frankfurt in 1981

Along the years the Beetle was improved, and I was able to drive the new models and the non-Beetle VWs like the 1500 Variant, the 1600 Fastback and the 411/412—but this is purely a Beetle-Book—and I have sampled twin-carb., supercharged and otherwise souped-up Beetles. It was magic while it lasted, even if I was branded pro-German and a non-patriot, in some quarters. VWs certainly shone in rallies, especially in the East African Safaris, winning in 1953 (with Alan Dix), in 1954 and 1957. And typically happy things, like when an owner ran a bearing on the eve of a Continental holiday and was promptly loaned a replacement Beetle by Mr. Graydon, enhanced VW allure. And on one of my visits to Plaistow I was shown a 1947 'split-window' Beetle, the one with the stubby gear-lever surrounded by an ash-tray, that had been badly damaged in an accident; its owner said the odometer had been round three times but he was having the car repaired, as he wouldn't want any other car. I retained a personal Beetle until the Issigonis Mini Minor arrived and had to be tried, followed by Morris 1100, Rovers, BMWs and the like. But whenever I now encounter a Beetle on the road the memories return. And VW longevity is proverbial, as Bob Wyse—who started his paper *Safer Motoring*, the 'Independent VW/Audi Magazine', after a visit to discuss it with me—and his 100,000 (mile) Club endorses. I gave up my first Beetle after some 80,000 miles, when it was still good for 38–40 mpg of Esso Mixture and was only just beginning to develop a thirst for engine-oil. Part of the fun stemmed from VW advertising, outrageous copy-writing drawing attention to every aspect of the Beetle's advantages over ordinary cars, even to denouncing it as ugly in one of them.

There was even the attempt to cross the English

Channel in a Beetle, laid on with notable courage by Comdr. Gordon Amer, appropriately ex-Navy, and Jerry Amor, of the London VW Sales Staff, in 1961. The VW sank near Dover, if anyone feels like a salvage job, but it was a great endeavour.

There had been some anxiety over carburettor icing in 1960 but this was overcome in the new 34 bhp Beetle introduced for 1961. The price of the de Luxe model was by then £717, although the Standard sedan cost only £702. The Convertible was priced at £766. I sampled one of the new models around Motor Show time in 1960 and saw 70 mph on the speedometer and 60 mph in third gear. The engine was stiff, the car having done a mere 1000 miles at the time, so the $33\frac{1}{2}$ mpg of petrol I obtained was notable. Some writers were apt to report poor acceleration and heavy fuel consumption from the Beetles they tested but I think this was often due to the London Press department sending us out with stiff engines, because they were keen to get early publicity for the newest models. A VW took a long time to free-off. I know I was impressed again, with this 1961 model over the high quality of the finish, both inside and out, and the 'splendid gear change'. I did, however, find the steering, now hydraulically-damped, heavier than on my 1955 Beetle. The absolute fuel-range, by the way, came out at 304 miles. Incidentally, I have heard that some of the good quality of the VWs of those days stemmed from former out-of-work German professors with high qualifications being so glad of anything they could get that they worked as Inspectors in the factory, and knew only one standard—the highest. . . .

And all the time subtle improvements were being made. Larger windows, more space within, 12 volt electrics, better lamps, bigger and much more powerful engines, even front disc brakes

*Full-circle! A VW Beetle
Convertible beside a VW
Golf with the same 'fresh-air'
body-style. The hood stowage
on both vehicles is typical of
the problem of folding down
the substantial 'tops' of such
four-seater cars*

(first on the 1500 Beetle in August 1966, on the 1300 in 1970). In 1950 the fan cooling the finned cylinders was given a thermostatically-varied intake to obviate over-cool running. The 5.00-16 tyres became 5.60-15 by late 1952. That year, too, synchromesh was used on the de luxe models, on all but bottom gear. A roll-back sun-roof was an optional extra and the typically German cabrio-limousine Beetle was a notable model, not to be confused with the openable Karmann Beetle. Mostly the changes were small and some were invisible, but important. The split rear window had gone by March 1953, the 1192 cc engine was standard for 1954, and twin chromium-plated exhaust tail-pipes replaced a single (usually rusty) pipe from mid-1955. Handling was enhanced by a front anti-roll bar in 1959–60 and the rear window had become really large by 1957–58. Power went up to 34 bhp at 3900 rpm for the 1961 model-year, with synchro-mesh now on all forward speeds. The Beetle road-holding was now deemed good enough for 1285 cc and 1493 cc engines, and the Super Beetle arrived in 1970, for 1971, endowed with 50 (DIN) bhp at 4400 rpm from a 1584 cc 7.5:1 compression-ratio engine. Detail improvements continued to be made and alongside the ubiquitous Beetle there were the VW pick-ups, vans, caravans, 'buses and other commercial vehicles, with under-floor engines of the Beetle type. Denis Jenkinson used one such pick-up for a time to carry his racing motorcycles and it proved very handy when I wanted to transport a 1927 Morgan 3-wheeler and a four-bladed wooden aeroplane-propeller from London to Wales. . . .

The staggering success of the once unwanted Volkswagen was built originally on a one-model policy, such as had served Henry Ford as well with his Model-T. Almost before Europe had cottoned-on, America, land of vast, soggy, multicylindered automobiles, went quite near to crazy over the, to them, quite minute Beetle—the indestructible little wonder car 'made by gnomes in the Black Forest'. Closer to home, I always thought that when Harry Ferguson was demonstrating the hill-storming abilities of his 4WD car to the Press he lost much of the impact by allowing a VW Beetle to perform very nearly as well! In the end VW production beat even the legendary 15 million of the Ford Model-T. Lack of space precludes a full breakdown of all the changes in VW Motors finances, directorships and changes of premises (the Ramsgate Distribution Centre, for example, was opened in 1964.) In 1979 production of the famous Beetle finally ceased at Wolfsburg. But it continues in Mexico, as Gordon Wilkins, sole survivor of those British motoring journalists who saw the advent of the VW in Berlin in 1939, was invited in 1981 to see for himself. And everywhere, in films, in books, on our roads (and in MCC trials, I would add) the Beetle appears, sleek, timeless, a member of a very memorable era of motoring history.

The fabulous, lovable, unique Volkswagen is refusing to expire—long live the Beetle.

Chapter 7
New Century, new Beetle

By the 1980s, and even though VW was quite ready to see the famous air-cooled Beetle given a dignified burial, the public would never let this happen.

Although Beetle production was down to 'only' 236,000 a year in 1980, demand continued strongly. Until and unless the Mexican factory became overcrowded with other VW models, the company was happy to churn out the air-cooled cars. As a business proposition, by this time in its existence the Beetle was almost uniquely profitable: not only that, but all over the world the 'aaahhh' factor (the sighs of affection which seemed to follow the Beetle everywhere) was a huge boost to the company image.

The 20 millionth car was built in Mexico in May 1981, the 21 millionth followed in June 1992, with annual sales actually beginning to increase again at this time. In Brazil, there was so much continuing interest that assembly of the 'Fusca', as the Beetle was called in that nation, was re-introduced in 1993, seven years after originally being written off.

Opposite Although its general proportions were the same as before, the New Beetle was modern in every detail. For 1998, there was no suggestion of separate bumper blades, and the long but shallow grille was needed to channel air into the front-positioned engine bay

Opposite *Once the cartoonists saw the New Beetle, it took them no time at all to turn the headlamps into eyes, and the grille into a wide smile. Quite like old times, really – but did you ever see wheels like this on the original Beetles?*

Even at the end of the 1990s, the latest Mexican-built air-cooled Beetles looked almost exactly as they had when German assembly of the cars had ended twenty years earlier. Nor had they changed much under the skin, for the standard engine was still the familiar air-cooled 1,584cc unit which produced a mere 44bhp, and braking was still by drums on all four wheels.

With a nod to modern times, however, from 1993 the engines had been fitted with electronic fuel injection, and a pollution-cleansing exhaust catalyst. Even so, in the face of whizz-bang claims from manufacturers all round the world, it was still a relief to find a simple, rugged, carefully-built car which needed only four speeds in its gearbox, and which could cruise endlessly at its modest maximum speed of 77mph, though it still took ages to get there.

The latter-day Beetle might now be one of the world's slowest cars, but it was also the world's best seller. No matter how you measured it (and rivals tried, in increasingly desperate ways...), Beetle sales of 21.5 million, and rising, were unapproachable.

Why not try again ?
Early in the 1990s, therefore, a few young people in VW's newest satellite design studio – in sunny California – settled down to think the unthinkable. If VW had done it once, could they do it again ? If the Beetle had been such a success in the twentieth century, could VW repeat the trick in the next ?

Back in Wolfsburg, top management knew what was going on, and did not discourage any pipe dreams. So, what if the Californian

Under that curvaceous retro-style skin, the New Beetle hid a front-engine/front-drive Golf platform. Although there was actually less space in the cabin than in that of the Golf, the New Beetle's hatchback made this a very versatile package

studio was coming up with weirde suggestions ? That was what 'think tanks' were all about. As other engineers have famously stated already – 'Paper is cheap, but cutting metal is expensive. Sketch as much as you like, but don't start building cars until we tell you'.

Like other car makers, VW had always been fascinated by North America – and particularly by California. Here there was wealth, here was a huge market, in most quarters there was no built-in barrier to new ideas – and VW had a great name on that continent.

Opening a new design studio in the Simi Valley, north of Los Angeles, VW therefore set its team to identify modern automotive trends, to work on draft design studies, and to see how VW could face up to the next legislative-limited century.

Whizz-kids, it seems, sometimes take longer to absorb self-evident truths than others who live in the real world. It was not until mid-1992 that the Simi Valley designers concluded that VW's North American reputation was still founded on the legend of the air-cooled Beetle, now a legend, and still being used in enormous numbers.

Reporting back to Wolfsburg, therefore, they made a momentous request – rather than developing cars with alternative power trains, rather than studying high-tech. batteries and electric power, and rather than building zero-emissions vehicles, why not produce an all-new Beetle instead ?

The New Beetle's facia was well-equipped, rounded in every aspect, and included air conditioning, a radio, cup-holders, twin safety airbags – and a flower vase, just for fun! All rather different from the late-1930s type

It's only if you look very carefully that you can see the suggestion of a front-mounted engine in the New Beetle, for the bonnet is a touch more bulbous than it otherwise might have been – and there is absolutely no space to mount an engine in the rear of this body. Cast alumniunium wheels were standard on all original 1998 models

From Wolfsburg, it seems, there was at first a stunned silence, but by 1993 approval had been given for a design study to be made. Quarter-scale models were available by May 1993, approval for a prototype followed – and the Board asked for a concept car to be ready for the 1994 Detroit Auto Show.

When unveiled in January 1994, 'Concept 1' caused a sensation. Styled by J.Mays (who would be running Ford's world-wide design efforts by the end of the 1990s), here was a brand new machine which carried all the characteristics of a Beetle, but without a single carryover part.

Visually, it was an amazing effort, for in every way it could only have been evolved by VW. It may have been smaller, rounder, heavier though aerodynamically more sleek than the original car, but here was a Beetle for the next century.

Although this car had been shaped sixty years after the original, the stance, bulbous and without a straight-line in sight, had been carried over, complete. There were arcs everywhere, inside and out, and not a harsh junction to be seen. As ever, it had a classic Beetle-type outline, with a sloping nose, the familiar hump-backed profile and a sloping

Seat styling suggests space in the rear of the New Beetle for just two people. As on the original type, passenger headroom is a problem for tall people

127

Even by the end of the first season, the New Beetle was available with a choice of three different engines – the four-cyl. 2-litre petrol (this), a 1.9-litre turbo-diesel, and even a 150bhp/2.3-litre narrow-angle V5 petrol type. More were expected to join in during the model's life.

tail, the headlamps were faired neatly into the front wings, and it was a two-door car with four seats. In the modern style, there were no separate bumpers, and to give it that authentic retro-look, 17 inch road wheels were fitted.

Except for one basic, and very important, difference – that it had front-wheel-drive, with a water-cooled engine – it all sounded very cosy and predictable. The very first example – the only example, let's be honest – was nicely finished in primrose yellow, and was built up on the platform of the next-generation Polo. Although VW talked ifs, buts and maybes about motive power at this time (including the options of electric or even hybrid diesel/electric – both of which might become important to the USA market in the 2000s), the original Concept 1 was fitted merely with an electric golf cart engine so that it could be moved around !

Concept 1, along with the suggestion that

up to 200,000 cars a car could be built, was only a coat-trailing exercise, and one which succeeded beyond all measure. Within hours of the car being seen in Detroit, hundreds of potential customers had placed orders with their dealers – all round the world ! After a second car, this time a red Cabriolet, appeared at the Geneva Show in March, interest redoubled.

Within a year, this 'who don't we...?' exercise had been turned into a production-feasible project. Studied at length by VW's stylists, by market planners and, not least, by the money men, the decision was made to go ahead – but on a bigger and more spacious platform. The second version of 'Concept 1', shown at the Tokyo Motor Show in October 1995, had not only been re-shaped to incorporate 15in. road wheels, and to have more rear-seat space, but sat on a larger, Golf, platform.

The original Beetle was built down to a price, but the New Beetle was engineered up to a much higher standard, which explains the cast alloy wheels, and the very complete equipment package

Even so, there was no chance that a 'new Beetle' would be fitted with anything but existing transverse/water-cooled VW engines. Sentiment was all very fine, VW reasoned, but economic realities came first...

Only five months later, at Geneva 1996, VW finally told the entire story – they had decided that 'Concept 1' would go into production, that it would carry the proud name of 'New Beetle', and that it would be assembled at the Puebla plant in Mexico. By this time all mention of electric or hybrid engines had been suppressed – and it was clear that this car would effectively be an additional, re-bodied version of the fourth-generation Golf range.

After which everything went quiet, VW got on with the job of preparing to build the new Beetle in series, and rumours began to spread about the car's final sales-ready specification. Advance orders, in the meantime, mounted up, and it seemed certain that VW already had a success on its hands.

If, that is, they could continue to remind their public that this was going to be a very different type of Beetle from the popular old model which still refused to die. Let no one forget, they pointed out, that technology had moved on by half a century. Even with a diesel engine installed, the new Beetle would be able to reach more than 100mph, while a comfortable cruising speed (traffic laws permitting) would be at least 90mph. Build quality standards would be equally as high as of old, but this was a car which would come stuffed with mechanical goodies, would be a lot heavier than the early type and, frankly, would have many more safety features.

Above all, they kept repeating, this would

Far Left *A nice touch – if you rotated the familiar VW badge, the lockable fuel cap of the New Beetle was exposed*

Left *Open wide, please – the hatchback of the New Beetle raised to show, with the rear seat folded forward, just how much stowage space was provided in the New Beetle. This, of course, was never a feature offered on the original types*

be a modern front-wheel-drive car, as complex as its other Golf-based relatives, certainly not the sort of the car which could be fettled under a shady tree by peasant farmers, or many miles off the beaten track in South America.

On sale – at last

Well before the official launch, at the Detroit Auto Show of January 1998, the more excitable motoring writers were having a field day, and VW did nothing to cool them down. Rumours of cabriolets and other fringe derivatives were premature, but one conclusion, that the use of a Golf IV platform, and the proportions of its engine bay, meant that a whole range of VW engines – petrol and diesel, mundane and sporting – might, just might, become available.

When VW finally introduced the new Beetle, originally for the North American market, there was joy, enthusiasm, and relief

– but no signs of disappointment. The production car's style had been carried over
from Concept 1, virtually unchanged, the
choice of specifications was as wide as
expected, and all criticism of the use of a
front-drive platform had long-since died
away. The flavour was right, even if the
after-glow was bound to be different.

For the moment, at least, there was only to
be a two-door saloon, the decision on pro-
ducing a drop-top car being deferred until
the first huge rush of saloon-car orders had
been satisfied. As expected, the new car used
a unit-construction body/chassis structure,
based on the totally modern pressed-steel
platform of the latest Golf. At this stage,
therefore, it is instructive to compare a few
basic dimensions of the new 1998 car against
the last of the old Beetles:

	NEW BEETLE	OLD BEETLE
Layout	Front engine/transverse/ front-wheel-drive	Rear engine/ rear-drive
Engine power (bhp)		
– petrol	115	44
– diesel	90	N/A
Length (in/mm)	160.7/4081	159.8/4060
Width (in/mm)	67.9/1724	61.0/1550
Wheelbase (in/mm)	98.7/2508	94.5/2400
Weight (lb/kg) (petrol version)	2,708/1,228	1,808/820

In almost every way, of course, the New
Beetle was also More Beetle – faster, longer,
wider, more spacious, and a whole lot heavier.
Amazingly, though, the New Beetle was also
expected to be much more fuel-efficient than
the old.

Because VW was clearly looking at a sure-fire sales success (deliveries to USA buyers began almost immediately after the Detroit Show closed its doors, and waiting lists increased by the day), they had little need to show other than pictures, for the technical specification almost sold itself. It's important to realise, though, that (as the specification detailed on page 124 confirms) this was to be a thoroughly modern Beetle in every way.

The use of the latest front-wheel-drive Golf platform ensured that the handling would be secure, the ride soft, and the refinement guaranteed. A choice of four-cylinder engines – a 2.0-litre/115bhp petrol and a 1.9-litre/90bhp diesel, gave all the choice that was immediately needed, as did the option of a five-speed all-synchromesh manual gearbox or a four-speed automatic transmission.

All this, along with 205/55HR-16 tyres on cast alloy road wheels, disc brakes on all four wheels, and the sort of attention to ride quality, silence and refinement for which VW engineers were already famous, meant that the car's performance and road behaviour could be assured. Power-assisted steering, and four-wheel disc brakes, controlled by an ABS anti-lock feature, were all eons away from the original type.

Inside the car, there were no surprises for a modern car buff, for this Beetle came complete with a carefully trimmed cabin, reclining seats, air conditioning, a radio with six speakers, cup holders (for USA buyers, this was a must), anti-theft alarm system, central locking, twin air bags – and, of all whimsical fittings, a flower vase, just like the original !

With VW aiming to produce 100,000 New

Compared with the original type, the New Beetle's performance was in a totally different league. Even with the economical diesel engine option, it could reach more than 105mph/169kph. Top speeds of 130mph/209kph were forecast for the 2.3-litre V5-engined version

Beetles in the first year, and an annual 130,000 thereafter, there was every chance that waiting lists would continue, which explains why European sales did not start until the end of 1998, and why production of right-hand-drive cars was postponed until the end of the century.

Even so, to titillate the rubber-stripping, traffic-light drag racers of the world, VW held out the prospect of an even more powerful version – powered by their novel narrow-angle 150bhp/2.3-litre V5 – before long. Since the Golf was already available with eight different engines – 75bhp to 150bhp, with three of them being diesels – the scope for further complication was enormous.

Count Down to a new Beetle

January 1991: VW opened a new design studio in Simi Valley, California, USA.

September 1992: The Californian design studio began sketching possible versions of a 'New Beetle'.

May 1993: The original quarter-scale 'New Beetle' model was shown to the VW Board of Management.

January 1994: The Concept 1 'New Beetle' saloon appeared at the Detroit Auto Show, intended to be a rear-engined machine.

March 1994: The 'Concept 1' Convertible was shown at the Geneva Motor Show.

October 1995: A much larger derivative of 'Concept 1', ready for front-engine/ front-drive, was shown at the Tokyo Motor Show. This was a true 'New Beetle' prototype.
  Production design, using the Golf IV platform, was signed off, for assembly at the Puebla, Mexico, plant in 1998.

March 1996: A further-developed production-standard 'Concept 1' was shown at the Geneva Motor Show.

January 1998: The New Beetle production car was displayed at the Detroit Auto Show, with the first cars going on sale in the USA in the same month.

October 1998: International-specification versions of the New Beetle went on display at European Motor Shows. European sales began before the end 1998.

All that, of course, was for the future, which looked assured in 1999, but which might change a lot in the early 2000s. At first, no question, the New Beetle was one of those fashionable cars for which trend-setters were happy to pay a premium. In the future, though, would they be happy with the restricted rear seat space, or the tiny luggage boot ? Would they still be happy with front-wheel-drive ?

For the traditionalists, of course, the most intriguing questions were – would the New Beetle last as long as the original ? And would it ever approach the same massive sales figures ?

Tune in again, in 2040 or so, to find out...

Specifications

**1953–54 UK model
Standard saloon,
de Luxe saloon,
Cabriolet**
Engine

Four cylinder, horizontally-opposed four-stroke.
77 mm × 64 mm bore and stroke 1192 cc. (From 1131 cc.)
Compression-ratio 6.0:1. Push-rod-operated overhead
valves. Valve clearances (cold), inlets 0.004 in., exhausts,
0.004 in. Exhaust valves of high nickel-chrome alloy.
Camshaft driven from crankshaft by helical gears. Heat-
treated, counter-balanced crankshaft. Light alloy pistons
each with three rings. Lead-bronze big-end bearings. Air-
cooling by fan over finned cylinders, with thermostatic
control of air flow. Cooling fan driven from extended
generator shaft, both driven by a vee-belt. Full pressure
lubrication, Oil-pump driven from camshaft. Oil flow via
an oil radiator; which is by-passed when oil is cold. Oil
capacity, 4.4 pints, or 5.3 US pints. Solex 28PCI
downdraught carburetter fed by diaphragm fuel pump. Coil
and battery ignition, with centrifugal and vacuum control
of timing. Firing order 1,4,3,2. 6-volt, 70 amp. hr. battery
under back seat. Bosch VJN 4BR Mk.3 distributor.
Contact-breaker points open 7.5 degrees before TDC, with
a gap of 0.016 in, 14 mm plugs – recommended grades,
Bosch W175T1 or T!A, Bera K175 14u/2, Lodge HD14,
Champion L10 or AC44. PLug gap, 0.024 in.–0.027 in.
Starter, Bosch EED, 0.4hp at 6 volts.
Power output, 30 hp at 3400 rpm. Engine rear mounted,
floating on recessed flange of rubber-cushioned gearbox.
1954: Compression-ratio 6.6:1. 36 (SAE) 6 hp at 3700 rpm.

Clutch
Single dry plate. Pedal play half to one inch.

Gearbox
In unit with engine. Constant-mesh 3rd and 4th gears
without synchromesh on Standard model. Synchromesh
on 2nd, 3rd and 4th gears of de Luxe and Cabriolet. Spiral
drive pinion and ring gear. Four forward speeds and
reverse. Ratios: *Standard model*: 3.60, 2.07, 1.25 and
0.80:1. *De Luxe and Cabriolet*: 3.60, 1.88, 1.23 and 0.82:1.
Reverse, respectively, 6.60 and 4.63:1.

Rear-axle
Swing axle. Final drive ratio, 4.4:1. Oil capacity, 4.4
pints, or 5.3 US pints.

136

Chassis	Of pressed steel, with two-piece, spot-welded floor pan. Channel shaped centre backbone accomodating control runs and fuel line.
Front suspension	Independent, with two trailing arms and square-section torsion bars.
Rear suspension	Independent, swing-axle, multiple leaf torsion bars.
Shock absorbers	Hydraulic double-acting strut-type.
Steering	VW worm and nut, divided track-rod.
Wheels & tyres	Disc wheels, 4J × 15. 5.60 × 15 tyres. (From original 5.00 × 16) Pressures, 1/2 occupants, front 16 psi, rear 20 psi: 3 to 5 occupants, front 17 psi, rear 23 psi. Turning circle, 36 feet.
Brakes	Foot brake on all four wheels. Hand brake on rear wheels. Mechanical operation on Standard model, hydraulic operation on de Luxe and Convertible.
Fuel tank capacity	8.8 gallons, or 10.5 US gallons.
Wheelbase	7 ft $10\frac{1}{2}$ in.
Track	4 ft 3 in.
Length	13 ft 4 in.
Width	5 ft $0\frac{1}{2}$ in.
Height (Saloon)	4 ft 11 in.
Ground clearance	6.8 in.
Loaded weight	Saloon: 1110 kg. Cabriolet: 1160 kg.
Maker's performance figures	Maximum and cruising speed: 110 Km/h, or 68 mph. Fuel consumption: 38 mpg or 32 US mpg. Oil consumption, 0.03–0.1 litre per 100 km. Hill-climbing, 1st gear = 37 per cent gradient.

Subsequent major model changes

1955 Twin chrome exhaust pipes. Raised tail lamps. Reshaped fuel tank for increased luggage space. Gear lever moved forward and cranked. Easier access to heater-control knob. Front seats increased in width by $1\frac{1}{4}$ in. and given triple squab-adjustment. More rear-seat room. Improved steering-wheel. Sun-roof now of pvc.

1956 Improved heater ducts. Sound-proofing for engine compartment.

1957 Much larger rear window. Improved brakes. Treadle-type accelerator. Improved instrument panel and larger cubby hole. Leatherette upholstery replaced fabric. Better screen-wipers.

1958   Clutch spring strength increased. Better fan-belt. Chassis strengthened.

1959   De Luxe model has front anti-roll bar. Dished steering-wheel. Pull-out door handles. Minor improvements to seats. Dynamo output up to 180 watts from 160 watts. Direction-indicators self-cancel.

1960   Compression-ratio of de Luxe model raised from 6.6 to 7.0:1 34 (DIN) bhp at 3600 rpm. Hydraulic steering-damper. Synchro-mesh on 1st gear. Automatic choke. All models: reshaped fuel tank, flashing direction-indicators, visible brake-fluid level in reservoir. Slimmer gear lever. Screen washers of pump type (formerly spare-tyre pressure had been used!) External mirror, improved clutch and handbrake cables, door-keeps, more front leg room. Single heater vent in rear compartment, bonnet spring-loaded, and de Luxe models get worm and roller steering and fuel gauge in place of reserve tap. Engine cooling improvements. Cabriolet has larger rear window, and badge deleted from bonnet of de Luxe models.

1963   Vinyl upholstery, horn button in place of half-ring, cranked sun-roof replaced folding roof.

1964   1200A model with former engine but the hydraulic brakes and synchromesh gearbox replaces Standard model for 1965. All models have slimmer screen pillars, bigger screen, press-button bonnet-release, lever-control of heater, fold-forward rear-seat squab, etc.

1965   1200A available with 41½ hp engine to special order. 1285 cc engine with 7.3:1 compression-ratio gives 50(SAE) bhp at 4600 rpm, for 1300 model, and Cabriolet. Safety front-seat squab, improved front suspension, 1300 numbering on bonnet, stalk control of lamps dipping, turn-indicators and lamps flashing, reversion to half-horn-ring except on 1200A model.

1966   Improved heater, shorter bonnet, anti-burst door locks. New 1493 cc engine introduced, with 7.5:1 compression-ratio, giving 53(SAE) bhp at 4200 rpm. Front disc brakes. Wider rear track.

1967   Uprated 1200 model. External fuel filler. Revised headlamps. 12-volt electrics on 1300 and 1300 Beetles. Semi-automatic transmission for 1500 model.

1968   Bonnet release in dash cubby. Ignition switch on steering column on 1300/1500 models.

1969 Dual braking system used for 1200 model.

1970 New 1600 replaces 1500 Super, using 1584 cc engine with a compression ratio of 7.5:1, developing 60(SAE) bhp at 4400 rpm. With 1300 engine known as 1300S model. MacPherson strut front suspension, with coil springs. Semi-trailing-arm rear suspension, replaces swing axle. Bonnet more bulbous. Vertically-mounted spare wheel. 1300 engine gives 52(SAE) bhp at 4100 rpm. Larger drum front brakes on this model. Power of Super Beetle increased to 60 bhp.

1971 Computer diagnosis for 88 fault-finding checks on all models. 12-volt electrics on 1200 model.

1972 Curved windscreen. Restyled instrument panel with hooded speedometer. 1300 engine fitted to 1300A version of former 1200 model.

1973 'Big' Beetle introduced, with larger wheels and tyres (radial 175HR) and body changes, including imitation wood veneer on part of dash. Limited edition of GT Beetle, a 1300 with the 1584 cc engine, front disc brakes and other luxury items.

1974 New turn-indicators in front bumpers. Painted hub covers.

1975 Most models uprated and 1200L luxury version of 1200 introduced. Semi-automatic transmission discontinued.

1976 1303LS Cabriolet fitted with self-stabilizing steering, wide-rim wheels and heated back window.

The above are only some of the many changes and improvements made to the VW Beetle, but serve as identifying factors. These changes were mostly introduced in August of the years quoted, in readiness for the following model year.

Beetle production milestones (includes Beetle variants).

January 1948	20,000th.
March 1950	100,000th.
July 1953	500,000th.
August 1955	1,000,000th.
December 1957	2,000,000th.
August 1959	3,000,000th.
November 1960	4,000,000th.
December 1961	5,000,000th.

October 1962	6,000,000th.
September 1963	7,000,000th.
June 1964	8,000,000th.
December 1964	9,000,000th.
September 1965	10,000,000th.
April 1966	11,000,000th.
December 1966	12,000,000th.

New front-wheel-drive VWs were introduced in 1974 with the Golf. But the 'old' Beetle carried on regardless, and has now passed the 21 million mark.

Output Figures for Beetles and variants (not including commercials)

1945	1,785
1946	10,020
1947	8,987
1948	19,244
1949	46,154
1950	90,038
1951	105,712
1952	136,013
1953	179,740
1954	242,373
1955	329,893
1956	395,690
1957	472,554
1958	533,399
1959	696,860
1960	865,858
1961	1,007,113
1962	1,184,675
1963	1,209,591
1964	1,410,715
1965	1,542,778
1966	1,583,239

New-generation Beetle saloon, launched in 1998

Engine

Front-engine, front-wheel-drive layout, with engines transversely mounted. Unit-construction steel body/chassis structure, with two passenger doors and a hatchback.

Choice of engines, as in other VW Golf and Passat models:

Petrol powered. Four-cylinder, single-overhead-camshaft. 1,984cc, with 82.5mm x 92.8mm bore and stroke. Compression ratio 10.5:1. Fuel injection and catalytic converter.
Maximum power 115bhp (DIN) at 5200rpm
Maximum torque 125lb ft at 2400rpm

Diesel powered. Four-cylinder, single-overhead-camshaft. 1,896cc, with 79.5mm x 95.5mm bore and stroke. Compression ratio 19.5:1. Fuel injection, turbocharging, charge-air intercooler, and catalytic converter.
Maximum power 90bhp (DIN) at 3750rpm.
Maximum torque 154lb ft at 1900rpm

Petrol powered. Five-cylinder in narrow-angle (15 degree) vee, twin-overhead-camshaft. 2324cc, with 81.0mm x 90.2mm bore and stroke. Compression ratio 10.1:1. Fuel injection and catalytic converter.
Maximum power 150bhp (DIN) at 6000rpm
Maximum torque 151lb ft at 3200rpm

Transmission
In unit with front-mounted engines. Choice of five-speed manual, with synchromesh on all gears, or four-speed automatic transmission.

Chassis
Unit-construction steel body/chassis structure, using same basic platform as the VW Golf Series IV hatchback.

Front suspension
Independent, by coil springs, MacPherson struts (incorporating telescopic dampers), and anti-roll bar.

Rear suspension
Independent, by coil springs, torsion beam rear axle, trailing arms, telescopic dampers and anti-roll bar.

Steering
Rack-and-pinion, with power-assistance.

Wheels
Disc wheels, 6 1/2J x 16. 205/55R x 16W radial-ply tyres. Turning circle 35ft. 9in/10.9 metres.

Brakes
Disc brakes for all four wheels, with vacuum servo assistance. Hand brake operating on rear wheels.

Fuel tank capacity
12.1 Imperial gallons/14.4 US gallons/55 litres.

Wheelbase	98.7 in/2508mm	*Weight (Unladen)*	2,708lb/1,228kg (petrol version)
Track (Front)	59.4 in/1508mm	*Maximum gross weight*	3,638lb/1,650lb
Track (rear)	58.8 in/1494mm	*Claimed performance*	**2.0-litre petrol** Max speed
Overall length	160.7 in/4081mm	*figures*	115mph/185kph. 0–62mph 10.9sec.
Width	67.9 in/1724mm		**1.9-litre td** 106mph/171kph.
Height	59.0 in/1498mm		0–62mph 13.1sec. **2.3-litre V5 petrol** (est) 130mph/209kph.

141

INDEX

INDEX

Acknowledgements

William Boddy's personal VW Beetle story contains but only six of his own photographs. Not being a professional photographer and never having a camera always available to record the scene with his own humble Beetles, there has been no opportunity to show off what might have been a unique overview. Nevertheless, after much careful collection and selection the pictorial content of this book is undoubtedly a fresh visual insight into the traditional Beetle.

Grateful thanks are due to the late Robin Fry, acknowledged Beetle guru and then to Bob Shaill of the Split Rear Window (Beetle) Club of Great Britain. Others who supplied photographs are Mirco Decet, the late Michael Frostick, *The Garage and Motor Agent*, S. H. Grylls, Tim Parker Collection, Jerry Sloninger, W. H. T. Tayleur Ltd and a number of people whose photographs were not marked.

Obviously no book like this could be put together without the help of the Volkswagenwerk in Wolfsburg and their various agents throughout the world. Help did come from Germany itself, as it did from the British agency, that in the US and from the factory in Brazil. The publishers would like to thank VW UK for help with information on today's Beetle for this new edition. Pictures in chapter 7 were taken by Andrew Morland, or were supplied by the manufacturer.